Instant Pot R

ANTI-INFLAMMATION DIET RECIPES FOR ...

Anthony Marshall

Table of Contents

Introduction 1

What is Inflammation? 7

The Solution to Inflammation 11

How Some Diet Suppresses Inflammation 12

Food minimize inflammation 14

How Do You Know if You Have Chronic Inflammation? 16

Symptoms of Chronic Inflammation 17

Tests for Chronic Inflammation 18

Dangers of Chronic Inflammation 19

Autoimmune Disorders Associated with Inflammation 20

Degenerative Diseases Linked to Inflammation 22

A Mantra for Those with Chronic Inflammation 23

Diet and Chronic Inflammation 24

The Recipes That Helps Inflammation 28

Instant Breakfast Oatmeal 29

Pressure Cook Lentils Rice 30

Delicious Banana Nut Oatmeal 31

Pressure Cook Herb Potatoes 32

Great Homemade Baked Beans 33

Instant Pot Potato Salad 34

Slow Cook Strawberry Oatmeal 35

Delicious Carrot Potato Soup 36

Quick Quinoa Kale Salad 37

Instant Pot Creamy Rice 38

Instant Tasty Chickpea Stew 39

Pressure Cook Pea Spinach Pasta 40

Spicy Black Bean Quinoa Chili 41

Quick and Healthy Steamed Broccoli 42

Easy Baked Sweet Potatoes 43

Instant Gluten Free Lentil Tacos 44

Yummy Split Peas Soup 45

Easy Rice and Lentils Bowl 46

Hearty Spinach Lentil Soup 47

Yummy Mac and Cheese 48

Creamy and Delicious Potato Mash 49

Healthy Kale Lentil Soup 50

Quick and Cheesy Pasta 51

Healthy Tasty Roasted Potatoes 52

Creamy Mushroom Risotto 53

Quick and Easy Steamed Green Beans 54

Instant Spicy Jalapeno Rice 56

Quick Potato Chickpea Curry 57

Sweet and Sour Cabbage 58

Simple Spaghetti Squash 59

Slow Cook Stuffed Bell Pepper 60

Slow Cooked Tofu Broccoli and Zucchini 61

Instant Garlic Zucchini Noodles 62

Spicy Potato Corn Soup 63

Delicious Garlic Parsnip Gratin 64

Instant Pot Lime Rice 65

Green Beans with Mushrooms 66

Creamy Potato Leek Soup 67

Slow Cook Plain Garlic Rice 68

Healthy Red Beans with Rice 69

Easy Sweet Potato Gratin 70

Hot Ginger Carrot Soup 71

Instant Sweet Brown Rice 72

Pressure Cook Avocado Rice 73

Mushroom Barley Risotto 74

Delicious Sweet Potato Casserole 75

Millet Breakfast Porridge 77

Potato Carrot Corn Chowder 78

Sweet and Spicy Spaghetti 79

Pea Corn Herbed Risotto 80

Healthy Breakfast Quinoa 81

Instant Pot Apple Crisp 82

Great Garlic Tomato Beans 83

Creamy Coconut Squash and Apple 84

Slow Cook Split Pea Curry 85

Instant Split Green gram Rice 86

Simple Carrot Leek Potage 87

Pressure Cook Easy Pea Rice 88

Delicious Cauliflower and Broccoli Soup 89

Instant Onion Potato Soup 90

Bell Pepper and Pumpkin Soup 91

Cilantro Lime Cauliflower Rice 92

Delicious Refried Beans 93

Celery Tomato Bean Soup 94

Delicious Carrot Sweet Potato Soup 95

Gluten Free Minestrone Soup 96

Delicious Apple Cranberry Oats 97

Delicious Instant Applesauce 98

Breakfast Rice Pudding 99

Easy Steamed Brussels sprouts 100

Instant Garlic Chickpeas 101

Fresh Spinach Squash Risotto 102

Creamy Peach Oatmeal 103

Delicious Creamy Celery Soup 104

Pressure Cook Gluten Free Porridge 105

Instant Apple Squash Soup 106

Yummy Tomato Soup 107

Pumpkin Steel Cut Oatmeal.. 108

Gluten Free Creamy Polenta 109

Easy Black Bean Rice 110

Yummy Blueberry Oatmeal... 111

Simple and Quick Risotto 112

Instant Spanish rice 113

Slow Cook Plain Brown Rice 114

Gluten Free Coconut Oatmeal... 116

Delicious Vegetable Pasta... 117

Fast Vegetable Gumbo.. 118

Delicious Garlic Potato Mash 119

Instant Breakfast Quinoa 120

Slow Cook Maple Glazed Carrot 121

Instant Homemade Salsa... 122

Instant Spinach Artichoke Dip 123

Healthy Vegetable Stew 124

Slow Cook Spinach Lentil Curry.. 125

Delicious Almond Coconut Risotto 126

Instant Mixed Vegetable Curry 127

Delicious Potato Risotto 128

Instant Slow Cook Carrot Soup.. 129

Conclusion 130

Introduction

Acne, allergy, arthritis, asthma, autism, bruise, cancer, celiac disease, dementia, depression, dermatitis, diabetes, fatty liver, gingivitis, gout, hepatitis, high cholesterol, hyperacidity, hyperactivity, hypertension, infection, ingrown nail, injury, cirrhosis, lupus, nephritis, obesity, otitis media, painful bladder syndrome, stomach ulcer, stroke, swollen lymph nodes, tonsillitis, and urinary tract infection.

What do these conditions have in common? All of them are related to inflammation, whether as origin, contributing factor, and/or manifestation.

Examine yourself from head to toe, from outside to inside. Are you currently suffering from any of these conditions? Have you recently recovered from a condition in the list? Or do you find yourself experiencing a condition or two in a recurring manner?

Do you have a family history of any of those conditions? Do you have a loved one who is suffering from it, and you want to prevent it from happening to you as well? Are you already starting to feel initial symptoms of these conditions, and do you want to change your lifestyle habits before it gets worse? Are you just curious about anti-inflammatory diet, and are wondering if it is something that would fit and benefit your current lifestyle and preferences?

If your answer is yes to any of those questions, then this book is for you!

The anti-inflammatory diet is beneficial for the general populace. It is reminiscent of Mediterranean diet, and at the heart of these diets is the aim to promote healthier eating habits. And who would not benefit from making better food choices?

Before embarking on this diet though, consult with your doctor first, especially if you have an existing condition and if you are taking any medication, to ensure that your condition and/or medication do not react negatively with the anti-inflammatory food promoted in the diet. Consult your dietitian or nutritionist also if you are following a certain diet, whether for medical or personal reasons.

This book aims to serve as an introduction to inflammation and to the anti-inflammatory diet. This book will also giving you a whole lot of Instant Pot recipes to help you started on the journey towards health and wellness, placidity and vitality.

What is Inflammation?

Inflammation is the biological response your body goes into when dealing with harmful stimuli such as irritants, pathogens or even damaged cells. It is a self-protection mechanism that allows your body to begin the healing process. The 'hotness' or 'inflammation' you feel after you cut yourself or injure yourself is the result of your body working hard to heal itself. But what happens when your body experiences 'too much' inflammation?

A little inflammation is not a bad thing. In fact, when it happens, you should rejoice in knowing that your body is working tirelessly to correct the situation. However, like most good things, inflammation can get out of hand. When this happens, you may experience various health complications such as:

Weight Gain

Every day, thousands of people try to lose weight to no avail. They complain that they've tried out various diets but somehow none seem to be working. If they do find something that works, sooner than later, they are back to gaining the weight they thought they'd lost. This is because they neglect to look into inflammation as the cause for their weight gain. Inflammation contributes to weight gain in various ways. These include:

- If inflammation happens in the brain, it interferes with the functioning of the hypothalamus and this in turn increases your appetite and slows down your metabolism. When this happens, you will be eating a lot but burning up less energy, which leads to weight gain.

- Gut inflammation leads to leptin and insulin resistance. Leptin is the satiety hormone that tells your brain when you have had enough. When suffering from leptin resistance, you just eat and eat some more before leptin can communicate that you have had enough, which leads to weight gain. Another thing that gut inflammation does is to increase intestinal permeability. When this happens, more toxins will be able to permeate your bloodstream. Usually toxins are stored in fat cells to remove them from circulation. The more toxins you have, the more the fat cells expand to accommodate the more toxins leading to weight gain.

- Inflammation in the endocrine system suppresses adrenal and thyroid function. One of the main functions of the adrenal gland is to burn fat. Therefore, when you suppress the functioning of the adrenal gland, you are unable to burn fat, as you should leading to weight gain.

As you have read, inflammation is bad for you if you want to maintain the ideal weight.

Metabolic Syndrome

Metabolic syndrome refers to a group/cluster of lifestyle-related diseases including cardiovascular disease and obesity. They are clustered together because all of these diseases are linked to metabolic dysfunction. Markers of metabolic dysfunction include:

- Central obesity – this is excessive tummy fat
- Hyperinsulinemia – this refers to ongoing high levels of insulin
- Insulin resistance –your body loses sensitivity to insulin (you need more insulin to manage your blood sugar levels)

But the question is how these three factors are connected. Well, when on a diet high in carbohydrates, your blood sugar levels increase leading to high insulin levels to help blood cells absorb the glucose and thus manage your blood sugar levels. When you have high insulin levels, the production of cytokines (which are pro-inflammatory) increases and in turn this causes inflammation especially in predisposed persons. Once inflammation increases, it brings with it an increase in the production of free radicals. Free radicals affect cellular functions and one of those functions just happens to be insulin sensitivity. This is why chronic low-grade inflammation is linked to all three markers; that is, raised insulin levels, obesity and decreased insulin sensitivity.

Chronic Fatigue

Many people suffering from chronic fatigue have been told that the disease 'is all in their minds'. Fortunately, in recent years more researchers have begun looking into the association of chronic fatigue and inflammation. This is mainly because the two possess many similar symptoms including muscular pain and tenderness, sore throat, joint pain, swollen lymph nodes and sore throat.

As you know, inflammation is the way your body reacts to foreign particles. When you have symptoms of inflammation, it is safe to say that your body is fighting something even if that something is not yet known. This is why researchers link an overactive immune system to chronic fatigue.

Another thing that associates chronic fatigue with inflammation is the lack of cortisol in patients suffering from chronic fatigue. Cortisol is known to suppress inflammation. Thus, if your body has a cortisol deficiency, it will not be able to suppress inflammation and this will worsen symptoms of chronic fatigue. A dietary change often helps people suffering from chronic fatigue.

Some types of arthritis

When you hear the name arthritis, you automatically associate it with pain. Well, it is no coincidence since arthritis refers to inflammation in joints. When your joints experience inflammation, you will feel pain. The types of arthritis that have been linked to inflammation include:

- Gouty arthritis
- Rheumatoid arthritis
- Psoriatic arthritis
- Systematic lupus erythematosus

When you suffer from these types of arthritis, you may experience inflammation symptoms such as redness, joint stiffness, swelling of the joints, pain in the joints and loss of joint function.

It is important to note that inflammation does not have to be painful for it to be present. This is because many organs in your body just don't have enough pain-sensitive areas for you to feel that inflammatory sensation. This means that you can suffer from chronic inflammation over time without knowing, only for you to experience the effects of inflammation.

It is also important to note that various things can cause inflammation including:

- Processed foods high in sugar and unhealthy fats
- Omega-6 fats (and not enough Omega-3 fatty acids)
- Sleep deprivation
- Chronic stress

- Smoking
- Pollution
- Environmental chemicals
- Lack of exercise

Thus, chances are, if you experience any of the above things, you may be suffering from inflammation whether or not you experience pain.

The first thing you should do once you notice that you suffer from inflammation is not to reach for drugs because drugs just address the symptoms and not the root cause but rather to make some lifestyle changes. This is because most of the causes of inflammation can be addressed by making lifestyle changes like exercising more, reducing exposure to pollutants, not smoking and dietary changes.

In this book, we will focus on addressing inflammation by adopting an anti-inflammatory diet. Let us learn more about anti-inflammatory diet in the next chapter.

The Solution to Inflammation

An anti-inflammatory diet is a diet that is designed to reduce inflammation. Unlike most diets, it is not a one-size-fits-all diet. But it does include the dos and don'ts to guide you on how to proceed.

This means, it is up to you to check out the 'dos' or foods that have anti-inflammatory properties so that you can customize the diet according to your needs. For example, the diet recommends eating whole grains including wheat. However, some people don't react well to gluten. This means, they may not include gluten in their diet. However, they can certainly include other foods on the allowed foods list.

Other foods that have anti-inflammatory properties include fruits, vegetables, beans and foods that contain Omega-3s. You should also avoid foods that have inflammatory properties like highly processed foods, foods high in sugar and unhealthy fats.

It is important to point out that the anti-inflammatory diet is not a diet per say but rather a lifestyle change. You will be making a conscious decision to reduce the sources of inflammation. Let us learn more about how an anti-inflammatory diet will help address inflammation.

How Some Diet Suppresses Inflammation

It is important to understand how the anti-inflammatory diet works in order to be motivated to adopt the diet. Several related things affect inflammation. These are:

Free radicals

As you know, the human body is composed of cells. In turn, these cells are composed of molecules. The molecules consist of atoms. These atoms have elements joined by chemical bonds. The strength of the bonds determines the stability of the molecules.

Weak bonds often split leading to 'free radicals' that can quickly react with other compounds in order to gain stability. In the course of doing this, the free radicals can displace other molecules, 'stealing' their electrons and this can lead to a chain reaction that can cause disastrous effects by disrupting a living cell.

It is important to note that while free radicals are formed normally during metabolism, certain factors such as eating certain foods, daily stress, processed foods, smoking, pollution, drugs, some herbicides and radiation can also lead to the spawning of free radicals. When the free radicals become too many, it leads to oxidative stress.

Oxidative stress

Your body is built in such a way that it neutralizes and processes free radicals. Unfortunately, when the free radicals are too many, your body will be unable to neutralize them. It will become overwhelmed and this will create an imbalance. This imbalance is what it referred to as oxidative stress and it leads to inflammation.

Inflammation

Many experts suspect that oxidative stress is responsible for starting a bio-chemical cascade that leads to inflammation and other degenerative diseases. Remember I mentioned earlier that free radicals could overwhelm the system.

Think of your body like a computer. You can use it to perform many tasks. When you open one or two programs or documents, you have no trouble performing the tasks that will lead to getting the outcome you desire. However, what happens when you open 10 or more programs to deal with various tasks? Suddenly your computer becomes too slow. It becomes overheated.

The same can happen to your body if it has too many radicals. It becomes inflamed. When this happens, you will need antioxidants to bring down the inflammation. This is where the anti-inflammatory diet comes in.

Antioxidants

Antioxidants, which can be found in various antioxidant rich foods, work well to trap or neutralize free radicals. Antioxidants 'donate' their electrons such that free radicals are forced to bond to them. This stops the electron stealing reaction. It also protects cells from the damage caused by free radicals 'stealing' their electrons.

When free radicals are too many, they wreak havoc in your body. They cause damage and lead to oxidative stress, which leads to inflammation. Thus, neutralizing free radicals is the key to reducing inflammation. An anti-inflammatory diet contains many foods that are rich in antioxidants that can effectively reduce inflammation.

In summary, an anti-inflammatory diet does away with foods that cause oxidative stress while encouraging you to eat foods rich in antioxidants. When you follow this diet, you will effectively neutralize free radicals, prevent oxidative stress and consequently reduce inflammation. This is why it is important to know what to eat and what not to eat.

Food minimize inflammation

As we've seen, various things can trigger inflammation. There is no reason you should add on to this by eating foods that cause inflammation. In fact, by eating anti-inflammatory foods you can help your body deal with inflammation. Below are some anti-inflammatory foods that you should include in your diet

Fruits and Vegetables

Fruits and vegetables are rich in anti-inflammatory antioxidants and should feature prominently in your diet. Below are some of the best fruits and vegetables for treating inflammation:

Dark, leafy greens

Dark, leafy greens such as kale, romaine and spinach are great for reducing inflammation because they are rich in antioxidants. Kale contains quercetin and Kaempferol antioxidants while romaine contains carotenoids and spinach contains the antioxidant lutein. They are also equipped with other anti-inflammatory agents. You can enjoy such vegetables in salads and smoothies.

Blueberries

Fruits have anti-inflammatory vitamins, Vitamin A, Vitamin C and Vitamin E. These are great at helping your body repair itself. Blueberries also contain the powerful antioxidant anthocyanin, which is great for fighting inflammation. Eat the berries as a snack or add them to your salad and smoothies.

Cruciferous veggies

Cruciferous veggies such as broccoli, cabbage, kale and cauliflower are loaded with antioxidants such as lutein, zeaxanthin and carotenoids. This means they can successfully reduce inflammation and the symptoms associated with it. Make it a habit to increase your consumption of such vegetables. You can even include them in juices and smoothies.

Avocados

Avocados are great for reducing inflammation because they are high in carotenoids. Carotenoids fight inflammation. However, as always, you need to be careful when consuming avocados. Don't overdo it. Half a medium avocado per day should be enough for you. Anymore and you'll start adding on the pounds. You can eat it, as it is, add it to your salad or make guacamole if you'd like.

Asparagus

Asparagus is said to be a super anti-inflammatory food. This is because it has various anti-inflammatory nutrients such as asparanin A, quercetin, diosgenin, rutin, protodioscin, isorhamnetin, kaempferol and sarsasapogenin. Asparagus also has antioxidants. This makes it very useful in the fight against inflammation.

Beetroot

Beetroot is another important food you should include in your diet. It has anti-inflammatory benefits along other properties. Beetroot has phytonutrients such as isobetanin, betanin and vulgaxanthin that are linked to heart health. As you know by now, heart disease is also categorized as a symptom of chronic inflammation. You can include beetroot in salads and juices.

Herbs and Spices

Ginger

Ginger is a well-known spice among chefs. Apart from adding flavour to foods and tea, it is used for its healing properties. It contains anti-oxidants which are also good at fighting inflammation. You can sprinkle a dash of ginger onto your tea and soups whenever you like. This will increase your consumption of this useful spice.

Garlic

Garlic has been linked to various health benefits such as cardiovascular health and prevention of obesity and arthritis. It also has anti-inflammatory properties. Garlic contains the compounds thiacremonone and vinyldithin, which are good at inhibiting inflammatory messenger molecules. Allicin, a compound in garlic, also has many anti-inflammatory benefits. You can use garlic in various foods, salads and soups.

Turmeric

Turmeric is a chef's best friend because it not only adds flavour to food but it also adds colour. Another thing it is known for is its anti-inflammatory properties. You can put it in your vegetables and soup. But take note that turmeric is a bit pungent. If you're not used to it, start with using a little at a time and gradually increase the content.

How Do You Know if You Have Chronic Inflammation?

In her mid-forties, Susan began to feel less vibrant. The change came on her so slowly that it was months before she began to recognize that something had changed. One morning, getting ready to go to work, she realized she just wanted to go back to bed; then she realized she had felt that way more mornings than not, for months. She began to have rashes, for no apparent reason. She began to have trouble completing her sentences, trouble remembering the word she was looking for. Often, she felt she was just moving through her life as through a soupy fog.

She began to seek medical help. The first doctor told her she was fine, just anemic. Another physician told her there was nothing really wrong, she just needed a Vitamin D supplement. The "just" diagnoses continued, doctor to doctor – while Susan felt worse and worse all the time. It was six years – *six years* – before a physician diagnosed her with Hashimoto's Thyroiditis, an autoimmune disorder.

But that wasn't the end of Susan's struggle. The physician prescribed medication, which Susan took. She got worse instead of better, with joint pain, itching, and frequent bouts of dizziness. She began to feel that physicians and even friends and family doubted there was anything really wrong with her – that she was imagining her symptoms.

Like a lot of people with autoimmune, Susan never found a single physician, or a single treatment, that worked. And she never found a medication that really helped.

Instead, over the course of two years, she changed her food and lifestyle choices in a number of ways. She identified her food intolerances (gluten, corn and eggs) and – overwhelming as it seemed – began to eliminate them from her diet, for good. She increased foods high in fiber and antioxidants (such as eating blueberries). She ate probiotic foods and supplements. And she looked at the causes of stress in her life – like her job, and her mother – and, though it wasn't easy, she found another job that paid less but also stressed her out less. And she began, for the first time in her life, to draw boundaries with her mother.

And she got better. Slowly at first. Then one day, she realized how much better she felt than she had a year ago. She continues to improve. There are flare-ups in which the aches and the brain fog return, mostly during allergy season, when her immune system is in overdrive. But she's better, and she recognizes it. And that gives her the will to keep to her anti-inflammatory protocol, and continue to look for new solutions.

Symptoms of Chronic Inflammation

How about you? If you're reading this book, you probably suspect inflammation is a challenge in your life. How do you know for sure? See if the following symptoms or possible indications of inflammation sound familiar.

- Allergies and asthma – have you struggled with allergies or had issues with asthma since you were a child? Allergy and asthma are both closely connected to inflammation.

- Ongoing aches and pains – if aches in muscles and joints are a regular element of your life, your body is almost certainly inflamed. The cytokines your immune cells or fat cells are producing make you feel sore and ache-y.

- Brain fog – do you feel you've been losing your ability to think clearly – to find the word you're looking for, to multi task as effectively as you used to?

- Overweight – if you're overweight, your fat cells are producing more inflammation-causing chemicals.

- Fatigue – one man with autoimmune said he began to realize he climbed two flights of stairs when he got to work – and he was done for the day. He just felt he might as well go home and go back to bed. If you're feeling more fatigued, much more often, inflammation could have a role in your struggle. If your immune system is producing too many inflammatory chemicals and antibodies, you may feel like you do when you are fighting off the flu – because as far as your immune system is concerned, you are.

- Skin problems – rashes, redness and itching are signs of inflammation.

- Infections – if you have chronic infections like hepatitis, herpes or *Epstein barr* virus, your body is in immune overdrive all the time – and that means inflammation.

- Allergies – if you suffer with allergies, you have the classic symptoms of inflammation: redness, swelling and itching. Allergies are experienced in response to substances that are *not* toxic (like pollen and certain foods), but that your body *perceives* as toxic. Exposing your body to them results in an immune response, and inflammation.

- Chronic digestive problems – if you have irritable bowel syndrome, ulcers, or frequently experience bloating, gas or diarrhea, it's a sign your gut is out of balance, and that almost always means there's inflammation.

- Trouble sleeping – chemicals and substances produced as a result of inflammation are also associated with sleep disorders, and a UCLA study links sleep disorders with inflammatory markers.

- You've been diagnosed with an autoimmune disease – any autoimmune disease results in excessive inflammation.

Tests for Chronic Inflammation

If your doctor believes inflammation is a problem for you, he or she can order tests that indicate excessive inflammation. Two of the most common are called:

- C-reactive protein (CRP) – this is a blood protein that is considered one of the strongest indicators of inflammation. If your CRP level is high, it indicates inflammation, and possible heart problems, as well as inflammatory disease.

- White blood cell count – white blood cell counts increase in fighting infection. If your white blood cell count is high and there's no infection present, it can be an indicator of inflammatory disease.

Additional inflammatory marker tests include:

- SED rate – looks for clumping of red blood cells, indicating inflammation.
- Elevated HDL – inflammation impacts HDL levels, quality and effectiveness.
- Elevated blood glucose – the insulin resistance associated with elevated blood glucose also indicates inflammation.
- Homocysteine level – elevated homocysteine level in the blood indicates chemicals that increase inflammation.
- Elevated ferratin in the blood – when inflammation is present, ferratin levels rise.

Anti-inflammatory foods

Dangers of Chronic Inflammation

There's a wide range of effects that chronic inflammation can have for someone suffering from it. This chapter will cover what diseases could be associated with the inflammatory situation in your body. Don't freak out, it's very unlikely you will get most of these diseases.

I highly urge you to consult your local doctor or medical expert, in order to investigate your personal risks on the long term. In itself, inflammation is mostly harmless, but it could be an indicator for something more serious. Always make sure your medical condition is properly researched, if needed with a second opinion from a hospital expert. This book will not be able to indicate for you which diseases you could develop, or might already have developed. For this, a thorough personal medical examination is required.

Autoimmune Disorders Associated with Inflammation

With autoimmune, the body's immune response is in overdrive. With acute, healthy immune responses, the body creates inflammation as part of the healing process, but the inflammation ends once the danger of infection is past. For a variety of reasons, with autoimmune disorders, the inflammation is chronic.

Autoimmune disorders can include:

- Addison's Disease, caused by the adrenal's inability to produce enough hormone;
- Alopecia Areata, in which the immune system attacks hair follicles;
- Antiphospholipid Syndrome, a condition causing problems with the lining of blood vessels, and which can result in blood clots;
- Autoimmune Hepatitis, which attacks and destroys liver cells and can lead to hardening of the liver;
- Celiac Sprue-Dermatitis, a condition in which any gluten eaten results in damage to the small intestine;
- Chronic Fatigue Syndrome Immune Deficiency Syndrome (CFIDS), which results in extreme fatigue;
- Diabetes Type 1, in which the immune system attacks the cells that make insulin, leading to high blood sugar;
- Discoid Lupus, an autoimmune condition that can damage the joints, skin, kidneys, heart, lungs, and more;
- Endometriosis, in which the tissue that generally lines the uterus grows somewhere else in the body;
- Fibromyalgia, a chronic disorder that results in pain, fatigue, and tenderness;
- Grave's Disease, which causes the thyroid to overproduce thyroid hormone;
- Guillain-Barre, which causes the immune system to attach nerves in the brain and spinal cord;
- Hashimoto's Thyroiditis causes the thyroid to under produce hormone;
- Hemolytic Anemia, in which the immune system destroys red blood cells;
- Idiopathic Thrombocytopenia Purpura (ITP), in which the immune system destroys blood platelets needed for clotting;
- Inflammatory Bowel Disease, which causes chronic inflammation of the bowel. IBD includes Crohn's disease, and ulcerative colitis;
- Insulin Dependent Diabetes (Type I), in which the body does not produce enough insulin;
- Juvenile Arthritis, a type of arthritis that affects children 16 and under;
- Meniere's Disease, a disorder of the inner ear;

- Multiple Sclerosis, in which the immune system attacks nerve protective coating, and impacts the brain and spinal cord;
- Myasthenia Gravis, in which the immune system attacks muscles and nerves throughout the body;
- Pemphigus Vulgaris, in which the immune system attacks the skin and forms blisters and sores;
- Pernicious Anemia, caused by an inability to absorb vitamin B-12;
- Polymyositis and Dermatomyositis are inflammatory myopathies that cause muscle inflammation and weakness;
- Primary Agammaglobulinemic; A rare genetic disorder that harms the body's ability to fight infections;
- Primary Biliary Cirrhosis, in which the immune system destroys the liver's bile ducts;
- Psoriasis, in which new skin cells grow too fast and pile up on the surface of the skin;
- Rheumatic Fever, which may develop after a group A Streptococcus bacterial infection;
- Rheumatoid Arthritis, which attacks the lining of the body's joints;
- Scleroderma, in which connective tissue in skin and blood vessels grows abnormally;
- Sjögren's Syndrome, which targets the glands that make moisture, such as the tear ducts;
- Vasculitis, which affects the body's blood vessels;
- Vitiligo, which destroys the cells that provide skin coloration.

Degenerative Diseases Linked to Inflammation

In addition to autoimmune, a number of degenerative diseases have been linked to chronic inflammation, including:

- Alzheimer's disease
- Cancer
- Carpal tunnel
- Depression
- Kidney failure
- Myocardial infarction (heart attack)
- Osteoporosis
- Parkinson's disease
- Stroke
- Tooth decay

A Mantra for Those with Chronic Inflammation

So chronic inflammation is widespread; a growing condition, in Western culture; and a serious threat. Now the question that matters most: do you have chronic inflammation?

Diet and Chronic Inflammation

Studies are increasingly linking diet and choices around diet to the presence of chronic inflammation, from such sources as processed and refined foods, glutens, simple carbohydrates, lectins, saturated fats, omega 6 fatty acids, simple carbohydrates, alcohol and caffeine. Following are specifics about the factors in diet that contribute to chronic inflammation and the diseases associated with chronic inflammation.

Don't assume government regulations are protecting you from food additives in processed foods and fast foods. Pew Research found that eighty percent of the additives in food have not been analyzed regarding their impact on the human body.

Food Additives

A recent study in Israel associates the following food additives with, among other problems, intestinal permeability. When the intestines are more permeable (commonly referred to as "leaky gut"), the leakage is seen by the immune system as attack by foreign bodies. These additives have been shown to significantly affect that response:

Refined salt - Processed foods in the United States have twice as much refined salt as foods in other countries, so the finding that refined salt is one suspected cause of chronic inflammation is particularly significant. A Yale University team found that refined, processed and bleached salts increased the number of cytokines, which in turn affects the myelin, the sheath around nerve fibers, and disrupts messages between brain and body.

Sugars – Sugars contribute to digestive dysfunction and leaky gut syndrome, inflame the endocrine system, and spike insulin.

Emulsifiers – Emulsifiers make it possible to blend substances that generally don't blend – like oil and water – and keep them blended. They are thought to cause pro-inflammatory bacteria from the gut into the body, and produce intestinal inflammation.

Organic Solvents – solvents are used to extract or dissolve substances. They are used in insecticides and in food preparation. In foods, they extract oils from nuts, beans and seeds. Solvents disrupt the communication between brain and body, so the immune system receives false communication to continue attacking, or does not receive communication telling it to stop attacking.

Gluten – Gluten is a protein present in wheat, rye, barley, spelt, and other grains. For many, the immune system perceives gluten as a foreign substance, and becomes inflammatory. *Microbial transglutaminase* is a gluten-derived food protein that thickens and binds processed meat, fish, dairy and baked goods, and that has the same impact on inflammation as other gluten.

Nanometric particles – These are various additives that are thought to improve the uniformity and texture of foods, as well as its taste. Additives such as MSG, food coloring and aspartame are often perceived by the body as foreign substances (which they are), triggering an inflammatory response.

Lectins

Lectins are proteins that bind cellular sugars, keeping them from functioning. Lectins also cause the body to perceive such cells as being foreign, causing an immune system response and inflammation. Lectins are found in saturated fats, certain polyunsaturated fats, alcohol and caffeine, nightshades (tomato, potato and eggplant), gluten, beans and peanuts, dairy and eggs.

Omega 6 Fatty Acids

Omega 6 fatty acids over-stimulate the immune system. They are found in vegetable oils like soy oil, corn oil, and canola. Their impact is worsened when they are heated.

Simple Carbohydrates

Simple carbohydrates are starches and sugars that have a high glycemic impact, meaning they are absorbed into the blood stream quickly. They have been closely linked to development of insulin resistance, and to greater risk of cancer and heart disease. They are sugars (table sugar, corn syrup and honey) and grains (flours that are absorbed quickly into the blood stream).

Trans Fats

Deep fried foods, fast foods and commercially prepared baked goods generally have high levels of trans-fat, as well as hydrogenated oils, margarine and vegetable shortening. Trans-fats promote inflammation, insulin resistance and obesity.

Dairy Products

Yes – this is a painful piece of news for many people. Milk and other dairy are common allergens that can trigger inflammation in the form of cramps, constipation, diarrhea, skin issues, acne, hives and breathing difficulty.

Feedlot-Raised Meat, Red Meat and Processed Meat

Feedlot cattle and other animals are fed soy, corn and bean foods, which are high in Omega-6 fatty acids. Their meat has higher fat levels and contains the antibiotics and hormones they've been given – it gets passed right along to you. All these characteristics are associated with increased inflammation.

Red meat contains the molecule Neu5Gc, which the body responds to with antibodies that may trigger inflammation. Additionally, processed meats contain chemicals, additives and agents linked to cancer.

Alcohol

A high consumption of alcohol often inflames body organs and has been associated with increased risk of cancer.

Your Own Food Intolerances

Your body may respond to particular foods with an inflammatory response. Corn, shellfish, dairy, eggs, tomatoes and peanuts are the foods that most commonly trigger a response, and inflammation. Investigate elimination diets to test what foods may by triggering an inflammatory response in you.

Cooking with an Instant Pot.

What more often take you up to 4 hours of cooking and preparing for 1 meal now should be possible for you to make it in less than 10 min which is simply incredible. You can make several large meals in a very short time and the only thing that you will have to do to make them is to place some specific ingredients of a recipe in an the instant pot then you are free to do whatever you want during the cooking process, for the instant pot doesn't need you to check on it every once in a while, once the time is up release the pressure and get ready serve some heavenly cooked recipes that will blow your family and anyone who taste it's mind.

The best thing about the instant pot is that is serves as a multitasking pot that works as a rice cooker, slow cooker, pressure cooker...so instead of spending hundreds of dollars on different pots you can now spend few dollars on 1 instant pot and get the best of it.

The Recipes That Helps Inflammation

Instant Breakfast Oatmeal

Serves: 2

Preparation Time: 15 minutes

Ingredients:

- 1/2 cup steel cut oats
- 1/8 tsp ground nutmeg
- 1/4 tsp all spice
- 1 tsp cinnamon
- 1 1/2 cups water
- 1 apple, peeled and chopped

Directions:

1. Add all ingredients into the instant pot and stir well.
2. Seal pot with lid and cook on manual high pressure for 3 minutes.
3. Allow to release pressure naturally then open lid.
4. Stir well and serve with non-dairy milk.

Nutritional Value (Amount per Serving):

- Calories 140
- Fat 1.6 g
- Carbohydrates 30.4 g
- Sugar 11.9 g
- Protein 3.1 g

Pressure Cook Lentils Rice

Serves: 4
Preparation Time: 40 minutes
Ingredients:

- 1 1/2 cup brown rice
- 1 cup brown lentils, dried
- 3 garlic cloves, minced
- 1 large onion, chopped
- 1 tbsp. olive oil
- 1 tbsp. thyme
- 1 cup potato, diced
- 3 1/2 cups vegetable stock
- Pepper
- Salt

Directions:

1. Add oil, onion and garlic in instant pot and select sauté for 5 minutes.
2. Now add remaining ingredients and stir well.
3. Seal pot with lid and cook on high for 20 minutes.
4. Allow to release pressure naturally then open lid.
5. Serve warm and enjoy.

Nutritional Value (Amount per Serving):

- Calories 504
- Fat 6.2 g
- Carbohydrates 92.9 g
- Sugar 4.1 g
- Protein 19.5 g

Delicious Banana Nut Oatmeal

Serves: 4

Preparation Time: 20 minutes

Ingredients:

- 2 ripe bananas, mashed
- 2 cups quick oats
- 1 tsp cinnamon
- 1/4 tsp nutmeg
- 1 tsp vanilla extract
- 3 1/3 cups water
- 1/2 cup pecans, chopped
- 4 tbsp. maple syrup
- Pinch of salt

Directions:

1. Add mashed bananas, oats, cinnamon, nutmeg, vanilla, water and salt in instant pot. Mix well.
2. Seal pot with lid and select porridge function for 10 minutes.
3. Allow to release pressure naturally then open lid.
4. Add chopped pecans and maple syrup, stir well and serve.

Nutritional Value (Amount per Serving):

- Calories 265
- Fat 3.0 g
- Carbohydrates 55.3 g
- Sugar 19.7 g
- Protein 6.0 g

Pressure Cook Herb Potatoes

Serves: 4

Preparation Time: 25 minutes

Ingredients:

- 1 1/2 lbs. baby potatoes
- 1 cup water
- 3 garlic cloves
- 1 rosemary spring
- 5 tbsp. olive oil
- Pepper
- Salt

Directions:

1. Add olive oil in instant pot and select sauté.
2. Once oil is hot then add potatoes, rosemary and garlic and sauté for 10 minutes.
3. Add water and seal pot with lid and cook for 10 minutes.
4. Release pressure using quick release method then open lid carefully.
5. Transfer potatoes to serving dish and season with pepper and salt.
6. Serve warm and enjoy.

Nutritional Value (Amount per Serving):

- Calories 252
- Fat 17.7 g
- Carbohydrates 21.9 g
- Sugar 0 g
- Protein 4.5 g

Great Homemade Baked Beans

Serves: 4

Preparation Time: 50 minutes

Ingredients:

- 1 cup navy beans, dried
- 1/2 cup water
- 1/2 cup vegetable stock
- 4 tbsp. tomato paste
- 1/2 tbsp. balsamic vinegar
- 1/2 tbsp. Worcestershire sauce
- 1/2 tsp mustard
- 1/2 tsp pepper
- 1/2 onion, diced
- 1 tbsp. olive oil
- 1/2 cup tomatoes, chopped
- 1/2 tsp sea salt

Directions:

1. Soak navy beans for 8 hours.
2. Add olive oil in instant pot and select sauté.
3. Once oil is hot then add onion and cook until soften.
4. Turn off sauté and add vegetable stock.
5. Add all remaining ingredients into the pot and mix well.
6. Seal pot with lid and cook for 30 minutes then open lid and cook until liquid absorb.
7. Serve warm and enjoy.

Nutritional Value (Amount per Serving):

- Calories 233
- Fat 4.5 g
- Carbohydrates 37.5 g
- Sugar 5.6 g
- Protein 12.8 g

Instant Pot Potato Salad

Serves: 4

Preparation Time: 20 minutes

Ingredients:

- 1 1/2 lbs. russet potatoes, diced
- 2 tbsp. olive oil
- 2 tbsp. rice wine vinegar
- 1 medium onion, chopped
- 4 tbsp. parsley, chopped
- 1/2 tsp salt

Directions:

1. Place steamer basket in instant pot and pour 1 cup water.
2. Add potatoes in basket and seal pot with lid and cook on high pressure for 5 minutes.
3. Release pressure using quick release method then open lid carefully.
4. In a large bowl, combine together onion, vinegar, pepper and salt.
5. Add potatoes and parsley in bowl and toss well.
6. Serve warm and enjoy.

Nutritional Value (Amount per Serving):

- Calories 190
- Fat 7.5 g
- Carbohydrates 29.2 g
- Sugar 2.6 g
- Protein 3.2 g

Slow Cook Strawberry Oatmeal

Serves: 6

Preparation Time: 6 hours 10 minutes

Ingredients:

- 1 cup fresh strawberries, chopped
- 2 cups oats
- 3 tbsp. maple syrup
- 1 tbsp. vanilla extract
- 1 tbsp. coconut oil
- 3 cups almond milk
- 1/8 tsp salt

Directions:

1. Add all ingredients into the instant pot and mix well to combine.
2. Seal pot with lid and select slow cook function then cook on low for 6 hours.
3. Serve warm and enjoy.

Nutritional Value (Amount per Serving):

- Calories 439
- Fat 32.8 g
- Carbohydrates 33.9 g
- Sugar 11.7 g
- Protein 6.5 g

Delicious Carrot Potato Soup

Serves: 6
Preparation Time: 20 minutes
Ingredients:

- 3 cups potatoes, cubed
- 3 cups vegetable broth
- 1 medium onion, diced
- 1 tsp pepper
- 1 medium carrot, diced
- 2 garlic cloves, chopped
- 1 tbsp. olive oil

Directions:

1. Heat olive oil in instant pot.
2. Once oil is hot then add potatoes, onion and garlic. Select sauté for 4 minutes.
3. Seal pot with lid and cook on high for 10 minutes.
4. Allow to release pressure naturally then open lid.
5. Serve and enjoy.

Nutritional Value (Amount per Serving):

- Calories 106
- Fat 3.2 g
- Carbohydrates 15.7 g
- Sugar 2.4 g
- Protein 4.2 g

Quick Quinoa Kale Salad

Serves: 4

Preparation Time: 15 minutes

Ingredients:

- 1 cup quinoa
- 1 cup kale, chopped
- 1 1/2 cup vegetable stock
- 4 tbsp. edamame, cooked
- 1/2 tbsp. garlic salt

Directions:

1. Add quinoa, stock, kale and salt in instant pot. Stir well.
2. Seal pot with lid and cook on high for 8 minutes.
3. Allow to release pressure naturally then open lid.
4. Transfer quinoa and kale mixture into the mixing bowl.
5. Add cooked edamame and mix well.
6. Serve and enjoy.

Nutritional Value (Amount per Serving):

- Calories 197
- Fat 3.8 g
- Carbohydrates 32.3 g
- Sugar 0.9 g
- Protein 9.1 g

Instant Pot Creamy Rice

Serves: 2
Preparation Time: 25 minutes
Ingredients:

- 1 cup brown rice
- 3/4 cup onion soup
- 4 tbsp. vegan butter
- 3/4 cup vegetable stock

Directions:

1. Add all ingredients into the instant pot and mix well.
2. Seal pot with lid and cook on high pressure for 15 minutes.
3. Allow to release pressure naturally then open lid.
4. Stir well and serve.

Nutritional Value (Amount per Serving):

- Calories 591
- Fat 27.0 g
- Carbohydrates 78.2 g
- Sugar 2.4 g
- Protein 10.5 g

Instant Tasty Chickpea Stew

Serves: 4

Preparation Time: 30 minutes

Ingredients:

- 28 oz. chickpeas, soaked overnight
- 24 oz. tomatoes, chopped
- 1 tsp paprika
- 2 onion, chopped
- 3 tbsp. water
- 1/2 cup dates, pitted and chopped
- 1/4 tsp allspice
- 1/2 tsp ground cumin
- 1/2 tsp salt

Directions:

1. Add onion, water, all spice mix, cumin, paprika and salt in instant pot and select sauté function.
2. Sauté for 5 minutes, stir occasionally.
3. Add tomatoes, dates and chickpeas. Stir to combine.
4. Seal pot with lid and cook on high pressure for 20 minutes.
5. Allow to release pressure naturally then open lid.
6. Stir well and serve.

Nutritional Value (Amount per Serving):

- Calories 841
- Fat 12.6 g
- Carbohydrates 149.3 g
- Sugar 42.2 g
- Protein 41.1 g

Pressure Cook Pea Spinach Pasta

Serves: 4
Preparation Time: 30 minutes
Ingredients:

- 1/2 lb. pasta
- 2 carrots, peeled and chopped
- 1/4 green onion, sliced
- 1/4 tsp red chili flakes
- 1 tsp ground ginger
- 2 cups baby spinach, chopped
- 1 cup peas
- 8 oz. mushrooms, sliced
- 3 garlic cloves, minced
- 3 tbsp. coconut amino
- 2 cups vegetable broth
- 1/4 tsp pepper
- 1/2 tsp salt

Directions:

1. Add all ingredients except spinach in instant pot and mix well.
2. Seal pot with lid and cook on high for 4 minutes.
3. Allow to release pressure naturally then open lid.
4. Add spinach and stir for 4 minutes.
5. Serve warm and enjoy.

Nutritional Value (Amount per Serving):

- Calories 246
- Fat 2.4 g
- Carbohydrates 43.3 g
- Sugar 5.0 g
- Protein 13.5 g

Spicy Black Bean Quinoa Chili

Serves: 6

Preparation Time: 25 minutes

Ingredients:

- 1/2 cup quinoa
- 14 oz. black beans, soaked overnight
- 14 oz. tomatoes, chopped
- 2 tbsp. tomato paste
- 4 cups vegetable broth
- 2 celery stalks, diced
- 1 tsp chili powder
- 1 tsp ground coriander
- 2 tsp ground cumin
- 2 tsp paprika
- 3 garlic cloves, minced
- 1 onion, chopped
- 3 sweet potatoes, peeled and diced
- 1 bell pepper, diced
- 1/2 tsp salt

Directions:

1. Add all ingredients into the instant pot and mix well.
2. Seal pot with lid and cook on high pressure for 12 minutes.
3. Release pressure using quick release method then open lid carefully.
4. Stir well and serve.

Nutritional Value (Amount per Serving):

- Calories 341
- Fat 3.3 g
- Carbohydrates 59.3 g
- Sugar 6.1 g
- Protein 21.0 g

Quick and Healthy Steamed Broccoli

Serves: 2

Preparation Time: 10 minutes

Ingredients:

- 1 lb. broccoli
- 2/3 cup water
- Pepper
- Salt

Directions:

1. Pour water into the instant pot.
2. Cut broccoli into florets and place on steamer rack.
3. Seal pot with lid and select steam for 2 minutes.
4. Allow to release pressure naturally then open lid.
5. Season with pepper and salt.
6. Serve warm and enjoy.

Nutritional Value (Amount per Serving):

- Calories 77
- Fat 0.8 g
- Carbohydrates 15.1 g
- Sugar 3.9 g
- Protein 6.4 g

Easy Baked Sweet Potatoes

Serves: 4

Preparation Time: 15 minutes

Ingredients:

- 1 lb. sweet potatoes
- 1 cup water

Directions:

1. Pour water into the instant pot then place steamer basket in the pot.
2. Scrub potatoes until skin clean completely then place on top of steam rack.
3. Seal pot with lid and select steam function and set timer for 10 minutes.
4. Allow to release pressure naturally then open lid.
5. Serve warm and enjoy.

Nutritional Value (Amount per Serving):

- Calories 134
- Fat 0.2 g
- Carbohydrates 31.6 g
- Sugar 0.6 g
- Protein 1.7 g

Instant Gluten Free Lentil Tacos

Serves: 4
Preparation Time: 25 minutes
Ingredients:

- 2 cups brown lentils, dried
- 1/2 tsp cumin
- 1 tsp garlic powder
- 1 tsp onion powder
- 1 tsp chili powder
- 1/2 cup tomato sauce
- 4 cups water
- 1 tsp salt

Directions:

1. Add all ingredients into the instant pot and mix well until combine.
2. Seal pot with lid and cook for 15 minutes.
3. Release pressure using quick release method then open lid carefully.
4. Stir well and serve.

Nutritional Value (Amount per Serving):

- Calories 354
- Fat 1.3 g
- Carbohydrates 60.8 g
- Sugar 3.7 g
- Protein 25.5 g

Yummy Split Peas Soup

Serves: 6

Preparation Time: 40 minutes

Ingredients:

- 1 lb. split peas, dried
- 1 medium onion, chopped
- 1 cup carrots, chopped
- 2 tsp paprika
- 7 cups water
- 2 tbsp. salt free seasoning
- 1/2 tsp pepper

Directions:

1. Add all ingredients into the instant pot and mix well until combine.
2. Seal pot with lid and select bean function for 35 minutes.
3. Allow to release pressure naturally then open lid.
4. Stir well and serve.

Nutritional Value (Amount per Serving):

- Calories 275
- Fat 1.0 g
- Carbohydrates 49.7 g
- Sugar 7.8 g
- Protein 19.0 g

Easy Rice and Lentils Bowl

Serves: 4
Preparation Time: 40 minutes
Ingredients:

- 1 cup brown lentils, dried
- 1 tbsp. thyme, dried
- 1 fresh rosemary spring
- 1 cup potato, peeled and diced
- 1 1/2 cups brown rice, uncooked
- 3 1/2 cups water
- 2 garlic cloves, minced
- 1/2 cup onion, chopped
- 1 tbsp. olive oil

Directions:

1. Add olive oil in instant pot then select sauté.
2. Once oil is hot then add onion and sauté for 5 minutes.
3. Add garlic in pot and sauté for minute.
4. Now add all remaining ingredients into the pot and mix well.
5. Seal pot with lid and cook on high pressure for 20 minutes.
6. Allow to release pressure naturally then open lid.
7. Stir well and serve.

Nutritional Value (Amount per Serving):

- Calories 482
- Fat 6.0 g
- Carbohydrates 88.7 g
- Sugar 1.8 g
- Protein 18.4 g

Hearty Spinach Lentil Soup

Serves: 4

Preparation Time: 35 minutes

Ingredients:

- 1 cup brown lentils, rinsed
- 5 cups spinach
- 4 cups vegetable stock
- 1/2 tsp thyme, dried
- 1/2 tsp turmeric
- 1 1/2 tsp ground cumin
- 2 tbsp. garlic, minced
- 1/2 cup celery stalk, chopped
- 1 large carrot, peeled and diced
- 1 small onion, diced
- 2 tsp extra virgin olive oil
- 1/4 tsp pepper
- 1/2 tsp salt

Directions:

1. Add oil in instant pot then select sauté.
2. Once oil is hot then add onion, celery, carrots and sauté for 5 minutes.
3. Add thyme, turmeric, cumin, garlic, pepper and salt and stir for 1 minute.
4. Pour vegetable stock in pot. Stir well.
5. Add lentils and stir for minute.
6. Seal pot with lid and cook on high pressure for 12 minutes.
7. Release pressure using quick release method then open lid carefully.
8. Add spinach and stir well.
9. Serve warm and enjoy.

Nutritional Value (Amount per Serving):

- Calories 225
- Fat 3.3 g
- Carbohydrates 36.1 g
- Sugar 3.0 g
- Protein 14.3 g

Yummy Mac and Cheese

Serves: 4
Preparation Time: 20 minutes
Ingredients:

- 2 cups noodles, gluten free
- 4 tbsp. vegan butter
- 2 cups cheddar cheese, shredded
- 1 cup heavy cream
- 1 cup vegetable broth
- Pepper
- Salt

Directions:

1. Add cream, noodles and vegetable broth in instant pot.
2. Seal pot with lid and cook for 7 minutes.
3. Release pressure using quick release method then open lid carefully.
4. Add butter, cheese and stir until melted.
5. Season with pepper and salt.
6. Serve and enjoy.

Nutritional Value (Amount per Serving):

- Calories 553
- Fat 43.3 g
- Carbohydrates 21.9 g
- Sugar 0.8 g
- Protein 19.7 g

Creamy and Delicious Potato Mash

Serves: 6

Preparation Time: 15 minutes

Ingredients:

- 3 lbs. potatoes, clean and diced
- 4 tbsp. half and half
- 2 tbsp. vegan butter
- 1 cup vegetable broth
- 1/4 tsp pepper
- 3/4 tsp salt

Directions:

1. Place steamer rack in the instant pot then pour vegetable broth.
2. Add potatoes and seal pot with lid.
3. Cook on manual high pressure for 8 minutes.
4. Release pressure using quick release method then open lid carefully.
5. Transfer potatoes in large mixing bowl and mash with masher.
6. Add half and half, butter, pepper and salt. Mix well until combine.
7. Serve hot and enjoy.

Nutritional Value (Amount per Serving):

- Calories 210
- Fat 5.5 g
- Carbohydrates 36.3 g
- Sugar 2.8 g
- Protein 5.0 g

Healthy Kale Lentil Soup

Serves: 4

Preparation Time: 30 minutes

Ingredients:

- 2 kale stems, chopped
- 1 cup lentils
- 1 sweet potato, diced
- 1 bay leaf
- 4 cups vegetable stock
- 2 garlic cloves, minced
- 1 small onion, diced
- 2 carrots, diced
- 1 tsp salt

Directions:

1. Add in instant pot lentils, garlic, onion, carrots and sweet potato, bay leaf and vegetable stock.
2. Seal pot with lid and cook on manual high pressure for 20 minutes.
3. Release pressure using quick release method then open lid carefully.
4. Add chopped kale and salt in pot and stir for 2 to 3 minutes.
5. Serve and enjoy.

Nutritional Value (Amount per Serving):

- Calories 231
- Fat 0.8 g
- Carbohydrates 41.9 g
- Sugar 6.7 g
- Protein 14.4 g

Quick and Cheesy Pasta

Serves: 6
Preparation Time: 15 minutes
Ingredients:

- 1 lb. pasta
- 1 cup half and half
- 15 oz. broccoli, frozen
- 15 oz. vegan cheddar cheese, shredded
- 4 cups water

Directions:

1. Add pasta, broccoli and water in instant pot and stir well.
2. Seal pot with lid and cook on high pressure for 4 minutes.
3. Release pressure using quick release method then open lid carefully.
4. Now select sauté function and add cheese and milk. Stir until cheese is melted.
5. Serve and enjoy.

Nutritional Value (Amount per Serving):

- Calories 580
- Fat 30.1 g
- Carbohydrates 48.7 g
- Sugar 1.6 g
- Protein 29.4 g

Healthy Tasty Roasted Potatoes

Serves: 4

Preparation Time: 20 minutes

Ingredients:

- 1 1/2 lbs. russet potatoes, cut into wedges
- 1 cup vegetable broth
- 1/4 tsp paprika
- 1 tsp garlic powder
- 1/2 tsp onion powder
- 4 tbsp. olive oil
- 1/4 tsp pepper
- 1 tsp sea salt

Directions:

1. Add olive in instant pot and select sauté.
2. Once oil is hot then add potatoes and cook for 5 to 6 minutes.
3. Add remaining ingredients into the pot and mix well.
4. Seal pot with lid and cook for 6 minutes.
5. Release pressure using quick release method then open lid carefully.
6. Serve hot and enjoy.

Nutritional Value (Amount per Serving):

- Calories 251
- Fat 14.5 g
- Carbohydrates 27.8 g
- Sugar 2.4 g
- Protein 4.2 g

Creamy Mushroom Risotto

Serves: 4

Preparation Time: 30 minutes

Ingredients:

- 2 cups Arborio rice
- 2 tsp extra virgin olive oil
- 1 tbsp. vegan butter
- 1 cup vegan parmesan cheese, grated
- 4 cups vegetable stock
- 4 tbsp. red wine
- 1 fresh thyme springs
- 3 cups mushrooms, sliced
- 1 medium onion, diced
- Pepper
- Salt

Directions:

1. Add olive oil in instant pot and select sauté.
2. Once oil is hot then adds onion and sauté until soften.
3. Add mushrooms and thyme and cook until soften.
4. Add rice and stir for minutes.
5. Pour vegetable stock and red wine in instant pot.
6. Season with pepper and salt.
7. Seal pot with lid and cook on manual high for 7 minutes.
8. Release pressure using quick release method then open lid carefully.
9. Add butter and cheese and stir until melted.
10. Serve hot and enjoy.

Nutritional Value (Amount per Serving):

- Calories 618
- Fat 18.3 g
- Carbohydrates 84.3 g
- Sugar 3.8 g
- Protein 27.4 g

Quick and Easy Steamed Green Beans

Serves: 2
Preparation Time: 10 minutes
Ingredients:

- 1 lb. green beans
- 1 cup water
- Pepper
- Salt

Directions:

1. Pour water into the instant pot.
2. Add green beans in steamer basket and place basket in the pot.
3. Seal pot with lid and cook on manual high pressure for 1 minute.
4. Release pressure using quick release method then open lid carefully.
5. Season with pepper and salt.
6. Serve warm and enjoy.

Nutritional Value (Amount per Serving):

- Calories 70
- Fat 0.3 g
- Carbohydrates 16.2 g
- Sugar 3.2 g
- Protein 4.1 g

Healthy Steamed Asparagus

Serves: 4

Preparation Time: 10 minutes

Ingredients:

- 1 lb. asparagus, 1 inch snapped off
- 1 tbsp. onion seasoning
- 2 tbsp. extra virgin olive oil
- 1 cup water
- Pepper
- salt

Directions:

1. Pour 1 cup water into the instant pot then place steamer basket in pot.
2. Place asparagus into the steamer basket and drizzle with olive oil.
3. Sprinkle onion seasoning.
4. Seal pot with lid and select steam function for 2 minutes.
5. Release pressure using quick release method then open lid carefully.
6. Season with pepper and salt.
7. Serve and enjoy.

Nutritional Value (Amount per Serving):

- Calories 84
- Fat 7.0 g
- Carbohydrates 4.5 g
- Sugar 2.0 g
- Protein 2.4 g

Instant Spicy Jalapeno Rice

Serves: 3

Preparation Time: 25 minutes

Ingredients:

- 1 cup brown rice
- 1/4 cup tomato paste
- 1 onion, chopped
- 1 cup water
- 1 jalapeno pepper, sliced
- 2 garlic cloves, minced
- 1/2 tsp salt

Directions:

1. Add little oil and onion in instant pot and sauté for 3 minutes.
2. Add garlic and sauté for 1 minute.
3. Add brown rice, jalapeno, tomato paste and salt. Stir well.
4. Pour water and stir.
5. Seal pot with lid and cook on high pressure for 15 minutes.
6. Allow to release pressure naturally then open lid.
7. Serve and enjoy.

Nutritional Value (Amount per Serving):

- Calories 266
- Fat 1.9 g
- Carbohydrates 56.7 g
- Sugar 4.4 g
- Protein 6.3 g

Quick Potato Chickpea Curry

Serves: 4

Preparation Time: 15 minutes

Ingredients:

- 2 potatoes, peeled and cubed
- 1 cup chickpeas, cooked
- 1/2 tbsp. cumin seeds
- 1 onion, chopped
- 1 tbsp. extra virgin olive oil
- 1/4 tsp ground ginger
- 1 tsp ground coriander
- 1 tsp turmeric
- 1 cup tomatoes, diced
- 1/2 tsp salt

Directions:

1. Add oil, cumin and onion in instant pot and select sauté for 3 minutes.
2. Add ginger, coriander, turmeric, tomatoes, salt and potatoes and sauté for another 2 minutes.
3. Pour water into the pot.
4. Seal pot with lid and cook on high pressure for 5 minutes.
5. Release pressure using quick release method then open lid carefully.
6. Serve and enjoy.

Nutritional Value (Amount per Serving):

- Calories 311
- Fat 7.1 g
- Carbohydrates 52.4 g
- Sugar 9.1 g
- Protein 12.5 g

Sweet and Sour Cabbage

Serves: 4
Preparation Time: 20 minutes
Ingredients:

- 6 cups red cabbage, sliced
- 2 garlic cloves, minced
- 1 onion, chopped
- 1 tbsp. extra virgin olive oil
- 1 tbsp. apple cider vinegar
- 1/2 cup applesauce
- 1 cup water
- Pepper
- Salt

Directions:

1. Add oil in instant pot and select sauté.
2. Once oil is hot then add onion and garlic and sauté for 2 minutes.
3. Add all remaining ingredients and mix well.
4. Seal pot with lid and cook on high for 10 minutes.
5. Release pressure using quick release method then open lid carefully.
6. Stir well and serve.

Nutritional Value (Amount per Serving):

- Calories 83
- Fat 3.7 g
- Carbohydrates 12.6 g
- Sugar 7.6 g
- Protein 1.8 g

Simple Spaghetti Squash

Serves: 2

Preparation Time: 20 minutes

Ingredients:

- 1 spaghetti squash
- 1 cup water

Directions:

1. Pour water into the instant pot.
2. Place spaghetti squash on steamer rack and place rack in instant pot.
3. Seal pot with lid and cook for 12 minutes.
4. Release pressure using quick release method then open lid carefully.
5. Cut spaghetti squash and remove seeds.
6. Top with favorite sauce and serve.

Nutritional Value (Amount per Serving):

- Calories 35
- Fat 0.7 g
- Carbohydrates 7.8 g
- Sugar 0 g
- Protein 0.7 g

Slow Cook Stuffed Bell Pepper

Serves: 4

Preparation Time: 25 minutes

Ingredients:

- 4 bell peppers, cut off the top
- 2 tbsp. garlic powder
- 3 cups vegetable broth
- 1 cup vegan cheese
- 1 cup quinoa
- 1 cup white beans, soaked overnight

Directions:

1. Add vegetable broth, garlic powder, quinoa and beans in instant pot.
2. Seal pot with lid and cook on high for 8 minutes.
3. Release pressure using quick release method then open lid carefully.
4. Stuffed bell pepper with bean and quinoa mixture.
5. Clean instant pot.
6. Place stuffed bell peppers in instant pot and select warm for 6 minutes.
7. Serve and enjoy.

Nutritional Value (Amount per Serving):

- Calories 405
- Fat 4.4 g
- Carbohydrates 70.4 g
- Sugar 8.6 g
- Protein 23.4 g

Slow Cooked Tofu Broccoli and Zucchini

Serves: 4

Preparation Time: 6 hours 10 minutes

Ingredients:

- 2 block firm tofu, cut into cubes
- 1/2 cup broccoli
- 1 zucchini, cubed
- 1 tbsp. coconut sugar
- 1 tbsp. garlic powder
- 1/2 tbsp. pepper
- 1 tbsp. red pepper, crushed
- 1/2 cup apple cider vinegar
- 2 cups tomato sauce
- 1 tbsp. fresh ginger, chopped
- 3 tbsp. tamari sauce
- 2 tbsp. olive oil

Directions:

1. Add all ingredients into the instant pot and mix well.
2. Seal pot with lid and cook on low for 6 hours.
3. Serve with steamed rice.

Nutritional Value (Amount per Serving):

- Calories 162
- Fat 9.5 g
- Carbohydrates 15.3 g
- Sugar 8.7 g
- Protein 7.1 g

Instant Garlic Zucchini Noodles

Serves: 4

Preparation Time: 15 minutes

Ingredients:

- 3 zucchini, spiraled
- 1 tbsp. garlic powder
- 1/2 tbsp. pepper
- 2 cups vegetable broth
- 2 garlic cloves, chopped
- 2 cups carrots, spiralized
- 2 tbsp. olive oil

Directions:

1. Add all ingredients into the instant pot.
2. Seal pot with lid and cook on high pressure for 4 minutes.
3. Allow to release pressure naturally then open lid.
4. Serve hot and enjoy.

Nutritional Value (Amount per Serving):

- Calories 137
- Fat 8.0 g
- Carbohydrates 13.3 g
- Sugar 6.1 g
- Protein 5.2 g

Spicy Potato Corn Soup

Serves: 4

Preparation Time: 6 hours 10 minutes

Ingredients:

- 2 cups sweet corn
- 1 lb. potatoes, cubed
- 1 tbsp. garlic powder
- 1/2 tbsp. pepper
- 3 cups vegetable broth
- 2 garlic cloves, chopped
- 1 tbsp. cornstarch
- 3 tbsp. red pepper, crushed
- 3 tbsp. olive oil

Directions:

1. Add all ingredients into the instant pot and mix well.
2. Seal pot with lid and select slow cooker function for 6 hours.
3. Serve with rice and enjoy.

Nutritional Value (Amount per Serving):

- Calories 310
- Fat 12.8 g
- Carbohydrates 44.1 g
- Sugar 9.4 g
- Protein 9.5 g

Delicious Garlic Parsnip Gratin

Serves: 4
Preparation Time: 30 minutes
Ingredients:

- 3 cups parsnip, sliced
- 2 cups vegan mozzarella cheese
- 1 cup vegan cream cheese
- 1 tbsp. garlic powder
- 1/2 tbsp. pepper
- 2 cups vegetable broth
- 3 garlic cloves, chopped
- 2 tbsp. olive oil

Directions:

1. Add all ingredients in instant pot except cheese.
2. Seal pot with lid and cook on high pressure for 4 minutes.
3. Allow to release pressure naturally then open lid.
4. Add vegan mozzarella cheese and set pot to warm for 5 minutes.
5. Serve and enjoy.

Nutritional Value (Amount per Serving):

- Calories 206
- Fat 10.5 g
- Carbohydrates 21.7 g
- Sugar 5.7 g
- Protein 8.2 g

Instant Pot Lime Rice

Serves: 3
Preparation Time: 15 minutes
Ingredients:

- 1 cup white rice
- 2 tbsp. extra virgin olive oil
- 1 1/4 cups water
- 3 tbsp. fresh cilantro, chopped
- 1 tbsp. fresh lime juice
- 1/2 tsp salt

Directions:

1. Add 1 tbsp. olive oil, rice, water and salt in instant pot. Stir well.
2. Seal pot with lid and cook on high pressure for 3 minutes.
3. Allow to release pressure naturally then open lid.
4. In mixing bowl, combine together remaining oil, lime juice and cilantro.
5. Add rice in bowl and toss until well combined.
6. Serve and enjoy.

Nutritional Value (Amount per Serving):

- Calories 305
- Fat 9.8 g
- Carbohydrates 49.4 g
- Sugar 0.2 g
- Protein 4.4 g

Green Beans with Mushrooms

Serves: 4
Preparation Time: 25 minutes
Ingredients:

- 1 lb. green beans
- 1 1/2 cups mushrooms, sliced
- 1/2 cup pureed tofu
- 1 onion, chopped
- 2 tbsp. vegan butter
- 1 cup vegetable broth

Directions:

1. Melt butter in instant pot.
2. Once butter is melted then add onion and mushroom and sauté for 3 minutes.
3. Add vegetable broth, green beans and pureed tofu. Mix well.
4. Seal pot with lid and cook for 15 minutes.
5. Release pressure using quick release method then open lid carefully.
6. Stir and serve.

Nutritional Value (Amount per Serving):

- Calories 109
- Fat 6.2 g
- Carbohydrates 10.9 g
- Sugar 3.1 g
- Protein 4.2 g

Creamy Potato Leek Soup

Serves: 4

Preparation Time: 25 minutes

Ingredients:

- 2 medium potatoes, peeled and diced
- 2 1/2 vegetable stock
- 1 bay leaf
- 1/2 tsp oregano, dried
- 1 leeks, sliced
- 1 tbsp. olive oil
- 1/2 cup coconut milk
- 2 fresh thyme springs
- 3 garlic cloves, minced
- 1/2 tsp salt

Directions:

1. Add olive oil and leek in instant pot and select sauté for 1 minute.
2. Add salt and garlic and sauté for another 1 minute.
3. Add potatoes, vegetable stock, bay leaf, oregano and thyme. Stir.
4. Seal pot with lid and cook on high pressure for 8 minutes.
5. Release pressure using quick release method then open lid carefully.
6. Discard bay leaf and puree the soup using blender.
7. Add coconut milk and stir well.
8. Serve and enjoy.

Nutritional Value (Amount per Serving):

- Calories 190
- Fat 11.0 g
- Carbohydrates 22.1 g
- Sugar 3.2 g
- Protein 3.0 g

Slow Cook Plain Garlic Rice

Serves: 4
Preparation Time: 15 minutes
Ingredients:

- 1 cup rice, uncooked
- 1 1/2 cups water
- 1 tsp garlic, minced
- 1/8 tsp salt

Directions:

1. Rinsed rice and add in instant pot.
2. Add garlic, water and salt. Stir.
3. Seal pot with lid and select rice function.
4. Release pressure using quick release method then open lid carefully.
5. Fluff rice with fork and serve.

Nutritional Value (Amount per Serving):

- Calories 171
- Fat 0.4 g
- Carbohydrates 37.1 g
- Sugar 0.4 g
- Protein 3.1 g

Healthy Red Beans with Rice

Serves: 5
Preparation Time: 40 minutes
Ingredients:

- 1/2 lb. dried red kidney beans
- 2 garlic cloves
- 1 celery stalks, diced
- 1 bell pepper, diced
- 1 onion, diced
- 1/4 tsp pepper
- 5 cups rice, cooked
- 3 1/2 cups water
- 1 bay leaf
- 1/4 tsp dried thyme
- 1/2 tsp salt

Directions:

1. Add all ingredients except rice in instant pot and mix well to combine.
2. Seal pot with lid and cook on high pressure for 25 minutes.
3. Allow to release pressure naturally then open lid.
4. Discard bay leaf from beans and stir well.
5. Serve with cooked rice and enjoy.

Nutritional Value (Amount per Serving):

- Calories 845
- Fat 1.9 g
- Carbohydrates 175.1 g
- Sugar 3.2 g
- Protein 24.0 g

Easy Sweet Potato Gratin

Serves: 4

Preparation Time: 20 minutes

Ingredients:

- 1 lb. sweet potatoes, sliced
- 2 cups vegan cheddar cheese
- 1 cup vegan cream cheese
- 1 tbsp. garlic powder
- 1/2 tbsp. pepper
- 1 tsp chili powder
- 2 cups vegetable broth
- 3 garlic cloves, chopped
- 2 tbsp. olive oil

Directions:

1. Add all ingredients into the instant pot except cheese.
2. Seal pot with lid and cook on high pressure for 4 minutes.
3. Allow to release pressure naturally then open lid.
4. Top with cheese and set pot with warm function for 5 minutes.
5. Serve and enjoy.

Nutritional Value (Amount per Serving):

- Calories 227
- Fat 8.0 g
- Carbohydrates 35.2 g
- Sugar 1.5 g
- Protein 4.8 g

Hot Ginger Carrot Soup

Serves: 4

Preparation Time: 6 hours 10 minutes

Ingredients:

- 5 medium carrots, shredded
- 1 tbsp. garlic powder
- 1/2 tbsp. pepper
- 3 cups vegetable broth
- 1 inch fresh ginger, peeled and chopped

Directions:

1. Add all ingredients into the instant pot.
2. Seal pot with lid and cook on low for 6 hours.
3. Using blender puree the soup until smooth and creamy.
4. Serve hot and enjoy.

Nutritional Value (Amount per Serving):

- Calories 69
- Fat 1.1 g
- Carbohydrates 10.2 g
- Sugar 4.8 g
- Protein 4.7 g

Instant Sweet Brown Rice

Serves: 2
Preparation Time: 15 minutes
Ingredients:
- 1 cup brown rice
- 2 tbsp. maple syrup
- 1 1/2 cups water

Directions:
1. Add all ingredients into the instant pot.
2. Seal pot with lid and cook on high for 8 minutes.
3. Allow to release pressure naturally then open lid.
4. Serve warm and enjoy.

Nutritional Value (Amount per Serving):
- Calories 396
- Fat 2.6 g
- Carbohydrates 85.8 g
- Sugar 11.9 g
- Protein 7.1 g

Pressure Cook Avocado Rice

Serves: 3
Preparation Time: 25 minutes
Ingredients:

- 1 cup rice
- 1/2 avocado, flesh
- 1 1/4 cups vegetable broth
- 1/4 cup green hot sauce
- 1/2 cup fresh cilantro, chopped
- Pepper
- Salt

Directions:

1. Add vegetable broth and rice in instant pot.
2. Seal pot with lid and cook on high pressure for 3 minutes.
3. Allow to release pressure naturally then open lid.
4. Add green sauce, avocado and cilantro in blender and blend until smooth.
5. Add avocado mixture into the rice and mix well.
6. Season with pepper and salt.
7. Serve and enjoy.

Nutritional Value (Amount per Serving):

- Calories 311
- Fat 7.4 g
- Carbohydrates 52.8 g
- Sugar 0.7 g
- Protein 7.2 g

Mushroom Barley Risotto

Serves: 4
Preparation Time: 40 minutes
Ingredients:

- 1 cup barley
- 2 cups mushrooms, sliced and sautéed
- 1/4 cup white wine
- 3 cups vegetable stock
- 2 garlic cloves, minced
- 1 onion, chopped
- 1 cup dry wild mushrooms, soaked and sliced
- 4 tbsp. cashew paste
- 1/4 cup parsley, chopped
- 1 tsp fresh rosemary
- 1 tbsp. olive oil
- Pepper
- Salt

Directions:

1. Add olive oil in instant pot and select sauté.
2. Once oil is hot then add garlic, onion, pepper and salt, stir well and sauté for 3 minutes.
3. Add soaked mushrooms, rosemary and thyme. Stir.
4. Add white wine and cook until liquid absorb.
5. Add vegetable stock and barley in pot. Stir.
6. Seal pot with lid and cook on high pressure for 15 minutes.
7. Release pressure using quick release method then open lid carefully.
8. Add sautéed mushrooms, parsley and cashew paste, stir until combine.
9. Serve and enjoy.

Nutritional Value (Amount per Serving):

- Calories 232
- Fat 4.9 g
- Carbohydrates 39.8 g
- Sugar 2.7 g
- Protein 8.1 g

Delicious Sweet Potato Casserole

Serves: 4
Preparation Time: 30 minutes
Ingredients:

- 2 sweet potatoes, peeled and cut into 1/4 inch slices
- 1/3 cup pecans, chopped
- 2 tbsp. heavy cream
- 3 tbsp. coconut milk
- 1/8 tsp nutmeg
- 1/2 tsp cinnamon
- 1/2 tsp vanilla extract
- 2 tbsp. vegan butter
- 1 tbsp. flour
- 1/3 cup coconut sugar
- 1 tbsp. vegan butter
- 1/2 cup raw cane sugar

Directions:

1. Pour 1 cup water into the instant pot and place sliced potatoes onto the basket.
2. Place steamer basket on the bottom of instant pot.
3. Seal pot with lid and cook on high pressure for 8 minutes.
4. Release pressure using quick release method then open lid carefully.
5. Transfer potatoes in large bowl.
6. Add 1/2 cup coconut sugar, 2 tbsp. butter, nutmeg, vanilla and cinnamon. Mix well and beat with blender until smooth.
7. Add coconut milk and cream. Mix well to combine.
8. Pour mixture into casserole dish.
9. Combine together 1 tbsp. butter, flour, 1/3 cup raw cane sugar and pecans. Sprinkle evenly over the top of casserole.
10. Place trivet in instant pot.
11. Pour 1 cup water in pot and place casserole dish on trivet.
12. Seal pot with lid and cook on high pressure for 13 minutes.
13. Release pressure using quick release method then open lid carefully.
14. Serve and enjoy.

Nutritional Value (Amount per Serving):

- Calories 334
- Fat 14.3 g
- Carbohydrates 50.9 g
- Sugar 17.7 g
- Protein 2.4 g

Millet Breakfast Porridge

Serves: 4
Preparation Time: 25 minutes
Ingredients:

- 2 cup millet flakes
- 1 tsp ground cinnamon
- 1 tbsp. vegan butter
- 1 tsp vanilla extract
- 1 tbsp. coconut oil
- 3 tbsp. maple syrup
- 2 cups heavy cream
- 1 cup water

Directions:

1. Add all ingredients into the instant pot and mix well.
2. Seal pot with lid and cook on high pressure for 2 minutes.
3. Allow to release pressure naturally then open lid carefully.
4. Stir well and serve.

Nutritional Value (Amount per Serving):

- Calories 280
- Fat 25.6 g
- Carbohydrates 12.3 g
- Sugar 9.1 g
- Protein 1.2 g

Potato Carrot Corn Chowder

Serves: 4
Preparation Time: 25 minutes
Ingredients:

- 1 large potato, diced
- 1 cup fresh corn
- 1 garlic clove, minced
- 1 celery stalk, chopped
- 1 carrot, peeled and chopped
- 1 onion, chopped
- 1 1/2 tbsp. cornstarch
- 3 cups vegetable stock
- 1/2 tsp fresh thyme
- 1 tsp olive oil
- 1/4 tsp pepper
- 1/2 tsp salt

Directions:

1. Add olive oil in instant pot and select sauté function.
2. Once oil is hot then add garlic, celery, onion and carrots and sauté for 3 minutes.
3. Add stock, potatoes, corn and seasoning. Stir.
4. Seal pot with lid and cook on high pressure for 4 minutes.
5. Allow to release pressure naturally then open lid.
6. Combine together water and cornstarch. Whisk in potato mixture.
7. Set pot on sauté mode for 2 minutes.
8. Stir well and serve.

Nutritional Value (Amount per Serving):

- Calories 159
- Fat 1.8 g
- Carbohydrates 33.7 g
- Sugar 3.8 g
- Protein 4.0 g

Sweet and Spicy Spaghetti

Serves: 6
Preparation Time: 15 minutes
Ingredients:

- 1 lb. spaghetti
- 2 tsp dried basil
- 2 garlic cloves, minced
- 1 onion, chopped
- 2 tbsp. olive oil
- 2 1/2 cups water
- 15 oz. tomato sauce
- 3 oz. tomato paste
- 28 oz. tomatoes, chopped
- 1/4 tsp red chili flakes
- 1 tsp brown sugar
- 2 tsp dried parsley
- 1 tsp dried oregano
- 1/4 tsp pepper
- 1/2 tsp salt

Directions:

1. Add olive oil in instant pot and select sauté function.
2. Once oil is hot then add onion and sauté for 2 minutes.
3. Add garlic and sauté for minute.
4. Now add all remaining ingredients and mix well until combine.
5. Seal pot with lid and cook on high pressure for 5 minutes.
6. Allow to release pressure naturally then open lid.
7. Stir and serve.

Nutritional Value (Amount per Serving):

- Calories 325
- Fat 6.8 g
- Carbohydrates 56.9 g
- Sugar 10.1 g
- Protein 11.6 g

Pea Corn Herbed Risotto

Preparation Time: 15 minutes

Ingredients:

- 1 cup Arborio rice
- 1/2 cup sweet corn
- 1/2 cup peas
- 1 red pepper, diced
- 3 cups vegetable stock
- 1 tbsp. extra virgin olive oil
- 2 garlic cloves, minced
- 1 onion, chopped
- 1 tsp mix herbs
- 1/4 pepper
- 1/2 tsp salt

Directions:

1. Add olive oil in instant pot and select sauté function.
2. Add onion and garlic and sauté for 4 minutes.
3. Add rice and mix well to combine.
4. Now add all remaining ingredients and stir well.
5. Seal pot with lid and cook on high pressure for 8 minutes.
6. Release pressure using quick release method then open lid carefully.
7. Stir and serve.

Nutritional Value (Amount per Serving):

- Calories 260
- Fat 4.1 g
- Carbohydrates 50.2 g
- Sugar 4.9 g
- Protein 5.7 g

Healthy Breakfast Quinoa

Serves: 6
Preparation Time: 15 minutes
Ingredients:

- 1 1/2 cups quinoa, uncooked and rinsed
- 2 tbsp. maple syrup
- 2 1/4 cups water
- 1/2 tsp vanilla extract
- 1/4 tsp ground cinnamon
- Berries and slice almonds for topping

Directions:

1. Add water, quinoa, vanilla, maple syrup, cinnamon and salt in instant pot. Mix well.
2. Seal pot with lid and cook on high pressure for 1 minute.
3. Allow to release pressure naturally then open lid.
4. Stir and serve sliced almonds and berries.

Nutritional Value (Amount per Serving):

- Calories 176
- Fat 2.5 g
- Carbohydrates 32.0 g
- Sugar 4.1 g
- Protein 6.1 g

Instant Pot Apple Crisp

Preparation Time: 15 minutes

Ingredients:

- 4 apples, peeled and chopped
- 1/2 tsp salt
- 1/2 cup water
- 1/2 tsp nutmeg
- 3/4 cup rolled oats
- 1/4 cup coconut sugar
- 1/4 cup flour
- 4 tbsp. vegan butter
- 1 tbsp. maple syrup
- 2 tsp ground cinnamon

Directions:

1. Add apples in the instant pot.
2. Sprinkle with nutmeg and cinnamon. Add maple syrup and water. Mix well.
3. Melt butter in bowl and mix together melted butter, brown sugar, salt, oats and flour. Add spoonful on top of apples mixture.
4. Seal pot with lid and cook on manual high pressure for 8 minutes.
5. Allow to release pressure naturally then open lid.
6. Serve with ice-cream and enjoy.

Nutritional Value (Amount per Serving):

- Calories 334
- Fat 13.1 g
- Carbohydrates 54.9 g
- Sugar 31.1 g
- Protein 3.6 g

Great Garlic Tomato Beans

Serves: 4

Preparation Time: 25 minutes

Ingredients:

- 2 tbsp. extra virgin olive oil
- 1 onion, chopped
- 1 lb. pinto beans, soaked overnight
- 1/2 tsp dried sage
- 1/2 tsp dried oregano
- 1/2 tsp garlic powder
- 14 oz. tomatoes, chopped
- 4 cups water
- Pepper
- Salt

Directions:

1. Add 1 tbsp. olive oil in instant pot and select sauté function.
2. Once oil is hot then add onion and cook about 5 minutes.
3. Add soaked pinto beans, water and remaining olive oil in instant pot and seal pot with lid then select bean/ chili function.
4. Release the pressure using quick release method then open lid carefully.
5. Add tomatoes, sage, oregano, garlic powder, pepper and salt. Mix well to combine.
6. Select sauté mode on low set timer for 15 minutes.
7. Serve warm and enjoy.

Nutritional Value (Amount per Serving):

- Calories 485
- Fat 8.6 g
- Carbohydrates 78.0 g
- Sugar 6.4 g
- Protein 25.7 g

Creamy Coconut Squash and Apple

Serves: 4

Preparation Time: 20 minutes

Ingredients:

- 1 lb. butternut squash, cut into cubes
- 2 medium apples, cored and sliced
- 1/4 tsp ground cinnamon
- 1/8 tsp ginger
- 1 cup water
- 2 tbsp. coconut oil
- 1 onion, sliced
- 1/4 tsp salt

Directions:

1. Pour 1 cup water into the instant pot and place steamer basket inside the pot.
2. Combine together apples, onion and butternut squash in steamer basket.
3. Sprinkle salt over the apple and butternut squash.
4. Seal pot with lid and select manual high pressure for 8 minutes.
5. Release pressure using quick release method then open lid carefully.
6. Transfer apple and squash mixture into the large bowl.
7. Using masher mash the apple and squash.
8. Add coconut oil, cinnamon and ginger in bowl and mix well to combine.
9. Serve and enjoy.

Nutritional Value (Amount per Serving):

- Calories 170
- Fat 7.2 g
- Carbohydrates 28.4 g
- Sugar 13.2 g
- Protein 1.8 g

Slow Cook Split Pea Curry

Serves: 4

Preparation Time: 20 minutes

Ingredients:

- 1 cup dried split peas
- 1 tomato, chopped
- 1/4 cup plain yogurt
- 1 tbsp. olive oil
- 1 red chili pepper, diced
- 1 tsp vegan butter
- 1 onion, chopped
- 1 garlic clove, minced
- 1/2 tsp garam masala
- 1/4 tsp turmeric powder
- 1/2 tsp dry mustard
- 2 tsp ginger, grated
- 2 cups water
- 2 tbsp. corianders, chopped
- 1/4 tsp asafetida

Directions:

1. Rinse split peas.
2. Add olive oil in instant pot and select sauté.
3. Once oil is hot then add asafetida and dry mustard. Stir for 50 seconds.
4. Add onions and garlic and sauté until onion soften.
5. Add all other ingredients except garam masala, corianders, salt in pot.
6. Seal pot with Lid and cook on manual high pressure for 10 minutes.
7. Release pressure using quick release method then Open lid carefully.
8. Add garam- masala and salt and stir well.
9. Garnish with chopped corianders and serve with rice.

Nutritional Value (Amount per Serving):

- Calories 237
- Fat 5.6 g
- Carbohydrates 35.1 g
- Sugar 6.0 g
- Protein 13.6 g

Instant Split Green gram Rice

Serves: 6
Preparation Time: 25 minutes
Ingredients:

- 2 cups rice
- 2 tbsp. fresh cilantro, chopped
- 1 tbsp. olive oil
- 1 tsp turmeric powder
- 1/2 cup Split Green gram (moong dal)
- 1 tbsp. vegan butter
- 2 cups vegetable stock
- 1/2 tsp salt

Directions:

1. Rinse both rice and moong dal. Drained.
2. Add butter and olive oil in instant pot and select sauté function.
3. Once oil is hot then add turmeric powder and stir for 30 seconds.
4. Add rice and moong dal in pot and mix well until well coated.
5. Add salt and vegetable stock. Stir well.
6. Seal pot with lid and select manual high pressure for 6 minutes.
7. Allow to release pressure naturally then open lid.
8. Garnish with chopped cilantro.
9. Serve warm and enjoy.

Nutritional Value (Amount per Serving):

- Calories 263
- Fat 4.7 g
- Carbohydrates 49.6 g
- Sugar 0 g
- Protein 4.5 g

Simple Carrot Leek Potage

Serves: 6
Preparation Time: 20 minutes
Ingredients:

- 1 lbs. potatoes, peeled and cubed
- 4 cups leeks, sliced
- 2 carrots, diced
- 5 cups water
- 1/2 tsp pepper
- 1/4 tsp salt

Directions:

1. Place carrots, potatoes, leeks, water, pepper and salt in instant pot.
2. Seal pot with lid and select manual pressure for 12 minutes.
3. Release pressure using quick release method then open lid carefully.
4. Using blender puree the soup until smooth and creamy.
5. Serve and enjoy.

Nutritional Value (Amount per Serving):

- Calories 144
- Fat 0.4 g
- Carbohydrates 32.9 g
- Sugar 4.7 g
- Protein 3.4 g

Pressure Cook Easy Pea Rice

Serves: 2
Preparation Time: 25 minutes
Ingredients:

- 1/2 cup rice
- 1/2 cup peas
- 2 cups vegetable stock
- 2 tbsp. vegan butter
- 1 onion, chopped
- 1/4 cup vegan parmesan cheese
- Pepper

Directions:

1. Add 1 1/2 tbsp. butter in instant pot and select sauté.
2. Once butter is melted then add onion and cook until soften.
3. Add rice and stir until slightly brown.
4. Add peas and vegetable stock and stir well.
5. Seal pot with lid and select manual high pressure for 8 minutes.
6. Allow to release pressure naturally then open lid carefully.
7. Add remaining half tbsp. of butter, pepper and parmesan cheese.
8. Wait for minute until cheese and butter melts.
9. Stir well and serve hot.

Nutritional Value (Amount per Serving):

- Calories 334
- Fat 12.6 g
- Carbohydrates 48.6 g
- Sugar 5.0 g
- Protein 6.8 g

Delicious Cauliflower and Broccoli Soup

Serves: 6
Preparation Time: 50 minutes
Ingredients:

- 1 lb. cauliflower, cut into florets
- 1 potato, peeled and chopped
- 1 1/4 cups broccoli
- 4 cups vegetable broth
- 1/4 tsp thyme
- 1/4 tsp pepper
- 1 tsp garlic powder
- 1 1/2 tbsp. apple cider vinegar
- 2 tbsp. fresh lemon juice
- 1/2 cup nutritional yeast
- 1/2 cup almond milk, unsweetened
- 1 small onion, chopped
- 2 celery stalks
- 1 cup carrot, shredded
- 1/4 tsp pepper
- 1/2 tsp salt

Directions:

1. Add potato, carrot, celery and cauliflower in instant pot.
2. Add vegetable broth and seal pot with lid and cook on high for 4 minutes.
3. Using blender puree the soup until smooth and creamy.
4. Now add all remaining ingredients and mix well to combine.
5. Select sauté function for 5 minutes or until broccoli is heated through.
6. Serve and enjoy.

Nutritional Value (Amount per Serving):

- Calories 274
- Fat 10.0 g
- Carbohydrates 32.5 g
- Sugar 7.8 g
- Protein 19.3 g

Instant Onion Potato Soup

Serves: 10

Preparation Time: 20 minutes

Ingredients:

- 5 cups potatoes, diced
- 6 garlic cloves, minced
- 1 cup onion, diced
- 8 cups vegetable stock
- 1 tbsp. season salt
- 1/4 cup vegan cheddar cheese, shredded
- 16 oz. vegan cream cheese

Directions:

1. Add vegetable stock, potatoes, garlic, onion and season salt in instant pot.
2. Seal pot with lid and select manual pressure for 10 minutes.
3. Release pressure using quick release method then open lid carefully.
4. Add cream cheese stir well until soup is well blended. Top with shredded cheese.
5. Stir well and serve.

Nutritional Value (Amount per Serving):

- Calories 228
- Fat 16.2 g
- Carbohydrates 15.1 g
- Sugar 2.0 g
- Protein 5.5 g

Bell Pepper and Pumpkin Soup

Serves: 6
Preparation Time: 15 minutes
Ingredients:

- 2 cups pumpkin puree
- 1/4 cup bell pepper, chopped
- 1/4 cup water
- 1/4 tsp nutmeg
- 1/8 tsp thyme, dried
- 2 cups coconut milk
- 1 onion, chopped
- 2 cups vegetable stock
- 1 tsp parsley, chopped
- 2 tbsp. cornstarch
- 1/2 tsp salt

Directions:

1. Add pumpkin puree, bell pepper, onion, vegetable stock, nutmeg, thyme, coconut milk and salt in instant pot and combine well.
2. Seal pot with lid and select manual high pressure for 6 minutes.
3. Allow to release pressure naturally then open lid carefully.
4. Mix cornstarch in water and add in pot then stir until soup becomes thicken.
5. Garnish with parsley and serve.

Nutritional Value (Amount per Serving):

- Calories 74
- Fat 0 g
- Carbohydrates 13.2 g
- Sugar 7.0 g
- Protein 6.1 g

Cilantro Lime Cauliflower Rice

Serves: 4

Preparation Time: 25 minutes

Ingredients:

- 1 lb. cauliflower
- 1 fresh lime juice
- 4 tbsp. fresh cilantro, chopped
- 1/4 tsp paprika
- 1/4 tsp turmeric
- 1/4 tsp cumin
- 1/2 tbsp. parsley, dried
- 2 tbsp. olive oil
- 1/4 tsp salt

Directions:

1. Wash cauliflower and cut into large florets.
2. Add all cauliflower florets into the steamer basket and place basket into the instant pot.
3. Pour 1 cup water into the instant pot.
4. Seal pot with lid and select manual for 1 minute.
5. Release pressure using quick release method then open lid carefully.
6. Transfer cauliflower into the plate.
7. Remove water from instant pot.
8. Add olive oil in pot and select sauté function.
9. Once oil is hot, add cauliflower florets into the pot. Using masher break cauliflower.
10. Add paprika, turmeric, cumin, parsley and salt and stir for 2 minutes.
11. Transfer cauliflower rice in serving bowl and add lime juice.
12. Serve warm and enjoy.

Nutritional Value (Amount per Serving):

- Calories 90
- Fat 7.2 g
- Carbohydrates 6.3 g
- Sugar 2.7 g
- Protein 2.3 g

Delicious Refried Beans

Serves: 4
Preparation Time: 40 minutes
Ingredients:

- 1 cup dried pinto beans, rinsed
- 1/2 tsp cumin, ground
- 1 tsp oregano
- 2 cups water
- 2 cups vegetable broth
- 1/2 jalapeno, minced
- 2 garlic cloves, minced
- 1/2 onion, chopped
- 1/2 tbsp. olive oil
- 1/4 tsp pepper
- 1/2 tsp salt

Directions:

1. Add olive oil in instant pot and select sauté function.
2. Once oil is hot then add onion, jalapeno and garlic and cook until soften.
3. Add all remaining ingredients and stir well.
4. Seal pot with lid and select manual for 30 minutes.
5. Allow to release pressure naturally then open lid.
6. Transfer bean mixture into the bowl and mash bean until smooth and creamy.
7. Season with pepper and salt.
8. Serve warm and enjoy.

Nutritional Value (Amount per Serving):

- Calories 212
- Fat 3.1 g
- Carbohydrates 32.9 g
- Sugar 2.0 g
- Protein 13.1 g

Celery Tomato Bean Soup

Serves: 4
Preparation Time: 15 minutes
Ingredients:

- 14 oz. white beans, soaked overnight
- 2 garlic cloves, minced
- 2 tbsp. extra virgin olive oil
- 14 oz. tomatoes, chopped
- 1 onion, diced
- 3 cups vegetable stock
- 2 celery stalks, diced
- 1 carrot, diced
- Pepper
- Salt

Directions:

1. Add olive oil in instant pot and select sauté.
2. Once oil is hot then add onion, carrot, garlic and celery and cook until soften.
3. Add tomatoes and stir well.
4. Add white beans and vegetable stock in pot.
5. Seal pot with lid and select manual high pressure for 10 minutes.
6. Allow to release pressure naturally then open lid carefully.
7. Season with pepper and salt.
8. Stir and serve.

Nutritional Value (Amount per Serving):

- Calories 411
- Fat 8.0 g
- Carbohydrates 64.1 g
- Sugar 4.0 g
- Protein 23.2 g

Delicious Carrot Sweet Potato Soup

Serves: 4
Preparation Time: 15 minutes
Ingredients:

- 2 lbs. sweet potatoes
- 2 carrot, diced
- 2 onion, sliced
- 1/2 cup almonds, sliced
- 1 cinnamon stick
- 1 tbsp. curry powder
- 1 tbsp. fresh ginger, grated
- Pepper
- Salt

Directions:

1. Add all ingredients into the instant pot except almonds.
2. Seal pot with lid and select manual high pressure for 6 minutes.
3. Release pressure using quick release method then open lid carefully.
4. Using blender puree the soup until smooth and creamy.
5. Garnish with sliced almonds.
6. Serve and enjoy.

Nutritional Value (Amount per Serving):

- Calories 311
- Fat 0.7 g
- Carbohydrates 73.4 g
- Sugar 5.1 g
- Protein 4.6 g

Gluten Free Minestrone Soup

Serves: 4

Preparation Time: 30 minutes

Ingredients:

- 28 oz. tomatoes, chopped
- 1 cup pasta, gluten free
- 1/2 cup fresh spinach
- 1 bay leaf
- 4 cups vegetable broth
- 2 cups cooked cannellini beans
- 1 tsp basil, dried
- 1 tsp oregano
- 2 garlic clove, minced
- 1 carrot, diced
- 1 onion, diced
- 2 celery stalks, diced
- 2 tbsp. extra virgin olive oil
- Pepper
- Salt

Directions:

1. Add olive oil in instant pot and select sauté.
2. Once oil is hot then add onion, garlic, celery, and carrot and cook until soften.
3. Add pepper, oregano and basil. Stir well.
4. Add tomatoes, pasta, bay leaf, spinach and vegetable broth. Stir well.
5. Seal pot with lid and cook on high pressure for 6 minutes.
6. Release pressure using quick release method then open lid carefully.
7. Add cooked beans and stir well.
8. Serve hot and enjoy.

Nutritional Value (Amount per Serving):

- Calories 463
- Fat 9.6 g
- Carbohydrates 69.1 g
- Sugar 10.1 g
- Protein 29.0 g

Delicious Apple Cranberry Oats

Serves: 6
Preparation Time: 50 minutes
Ingredients:

- 2 cups oats
- 1 tsp vanilla extract
- 4 tbsp. maple syrup
- 1/2 tsp nutmeg
- 1 tsp cinnamon
- 1 tsp lemon juice
- 2 tbsp. coconut oil
- 1 1/4 cup cranberries
- 4 medium apples, diced
- 3 cups water
- 2 cups almond milk
- 1/2 tsp salt

Directions:

1. Grease instant pot with coconut oil.
2. Add all ingredients into the instant pot except vanilla, maple syrup and salt. Soaked overnight.
3. Then add maple syrup and salt mix well.
4. Seal pot with lid and select porridge function.
5. Release pressure using quick release method then open lid carefully.
6. Add vanilla and stir well.
7. Serve warm and enjoy.

Nutritional Value (Amount per Serving):

- Calories 455
- Fat 25.8 g
- Carbohydrates 55.0 g
- Sugar 27.3 g
- Protein 5.9 g

Delicious Instant Applesauce

Serves: 4
Preparation Time: 20 minutes
Ingredients:

- 3 lbs. organic apples, peeled and diced
- 1/2 tsp ground nutmeg
- 1/4 cup water
- 1 cinnamon stick
- 1 tsp honey
- 1/8 tsp salt

Directions:

1. Add apples, nutmeg, water and cinnamon stick in instant pot.
2. Seal pot with lid and cook on high pressure for 5 minutes.
3. Release pressure using quick release method then open lid carefully.
4. Discard cinnamon stick and blend the sauce until you get desired consistency.
5. Add honey and salt to taste.

Nutritional Value (Amount per Serving):

- Calories 94
- Fat 0.4 g
- Carbohydrates 24.7 g
- Sugar 18.9 g
- Protein 0.5 g

Breakfast Rice Pudding

Serves: 6
Preparation Time: 30 minutes
Ingredients:

- 1 cup rice, rinse
- 1 tsp vanilla extract
- 1/8 tsp salt
- 4 tbsp. maple syrup
- 3/4 cup coconut cream
- 1 1/4 cups water
- 2 cups almond milk

Directions:

1. Add rice, maple syrup, almond milk, water and salt in instant pot. Stir well.
2. Seal pot with lid and select porridge function. It takes 20 minutes.
3. Allow to release pressure naturally then open lid.
4. Add vanilla and coconut cream and stir until well combined.
5. Serve warm and enjoy.

Nutritional Value (Amount per Serving):

- Calories 402
- Fat 26.5 g
- Carbohydrates 39.8 g
- Sugar 11.7 g
- Protein 4.7 g

Easy Steamed Brussels sprouts

Serves: 4

Preparation Time: 10 minutes

Ingredients:

- 1 lb. Brussels sprouts
- 4 tbsp. pine nuts
- 1 cup water
- olive oil
- Pepper
- Salt

Directions:

1. Pour water into the instant pot.
2. Add Brussels sprouts in steamer basket and place basket in the pot.
3. Seal pot with lid and cook on manual high pressure for 3 minute.
4. Release pressure using quick release method then open lid carefully.
5. Season with pepper, salt and olive oil.
6. Sprinkle pine nuts and serve.

Nutritional Value (Amount per Serving):

- Calories 107
- Fat 6.3 g
- Carbohydrates 11.4 g
- Sugar 2.8 g
- Protein 5.0 g

Instant Garlic Chickpeas

Serves: 2
Preparation Time: 45 minutes
Ingredients:

- 1 cup dried chickpeas, rinse
- 2 bay leaves
- 3 garlic cloves
- 4 cups water

Directions:

1. Add chickpeas, bay leaves, garlic and water in instant pot.
2. Seal pot with lid and select bean function for 35 minutes.
3. Allow to release pressure naturally then open lid.
4. Serve warm and enjoy.

Nutritional Value (Amount per Serving):

- Calories 371
- Fat 6.1 g
- Carbohydrates 62.1 g
- Sugar 10.8 g
- Protein 19.6 g

Fresh Spinach Squash Risotto

Serves: 4
Preparation Time: 25 minutes
Ingredients:

- 1 1/2 cups Arborio rice
- 3 cups spinach
- 1/4 tsp oregano
- 1/2 tsp coriander
- 1 cup mushrooms
- 1/2 cup dry white wine
- 3 1/2 cups vegetable broth
- 1 1/2 cups butternut squash, peeled and diced
- 1 bell pepper, diced
- 2 garlic cloves, minced
- 1 small onion, chopped
- 1 tbsp. olive oil
- 1/2 tsp pepper
- 1/2 tsp salt

Directions:

1. Add olive oil in instant pot and select sauté function.
2. Once oil is hot then add onion, squash, bell pepper and garlic and sauté for 5 minutes.
3. Add rice and stir until well combined.
4. Now add all remaining ingredients and mix well.
5. Seal pot with lid and cook on high for 5 minutes.
6. Release pressure using quick release method then open lid carefully.
7. Stir well and serve warm.

Nutritional Value (Amount per Serving):

- Calories 397
- Fat 5.4 g
- Carbohydrates 70.4 g
- Sugar 4.6 g
- Protein 11.3 g

Creamy Peach Oatmeal

Serves: 4
Preparation Time: 15 minutes
Ingredients:

- 2 cups rolled oats
- 1 tsp vanilla extract
- 1 medium peach, chopped
- 4 cups water

Directions:

1. Add all ingredients into the instant pot and mix until well combined.
2. Seal pot with lid and cook for 3 minutes.
3. Allow to release pressure naturally then open lid.
4. Stir well and serve.

Nutritional Value (Amount per Serving):

- Calories 173
- Fat 2.8 g
- Carbohydrates 31.3 g
- Sugar 4.0 g
- Protein 5.7 g

Delicious Creamy Celery Soup

Serves: 4
Preparation Time: 40 minutes
Ingredients:

- 5 cups celery, chopped
- 1/2 tsp dill
- 2 cups vegetable broth
- 1 cup coconut milk
- 1 medium onion
- 1/4 tsp salt

Directions:

1. Add all ingredients into the instant pot.
2. Seal pot with lid and select soup function.
3. Release pressure using quick release method then open lid carefully.
4. Using blender puree the soup until smooth and creamy.
5. Serve warm and enjoy.

Nutritional Value (Amount per Serving):

- Calories 189
- Fat 15.2 g
- Carbohydrates 10.2 g
- Sugar 5.2 g
- Protein 5.0 g

Pressure Cook Gluten Free Porridge

Serves: 2
Preparation Time: 25 minutes
Ingredients:

- 1/2 cup buckwheat groats, rinse
- 1/4 tsp vanilla extract
- 1/2 tsp cinnamon
- 2 tbsp. raisins
- 1/2 banana, sliced
- 1 1/2 cups almond milk

Directions:

1. Add all ingredients into the instant pot and mix well to combine.
2. Seal pot with lid and cook on high pressure for 5 minutes.
3. Allow to release pressure naturally then open lid.
4. Stir well and serve warm.

Nutritional Value (Amount per Serving):

- Calories 571
- Fat 44.0 g
- Carbohydrates 45.6 g
- Sugar 15.8 g
- Protein 8.5 g

Instant Apple Squash Soup

Serves: 6
Preparation Time: 25 minutes
Ingredients:

- 1 lb. butternut squash, peeled and cubed
- 1 tbsp. olive oil
- 4 cups vegetable broth
- 1 tsp ginger powder
- 1 medium apple, peeled and diced

Directions:

1. Add olive oil in instant pot and select sauté function.
2. Once oil is hot then add squash and cook for 5 minutes.
3. Now add all remaining ingredients and mix well.
4. Seal pot with lid and cook on high pressure for 10 minutes.
5. Release pressure using quick release method then open lid carefully.
6. Puree the soup using blender.
7. Serve warm and enjoy.

Nutritional Value (Amount per Serving):

- Calories 100
- Fat 3.4 g
- Carbohydrates 14.8 g
- Sugar 6.0 g
- Protein 4.1 g

Yummy Tomato Soup

Serves: 4
Preparation Time: 30 minutes
Ingredients:

- 28 oz. tomatoes, chopped
- 1 tbsp. balsamic vinegar
- 1 tbsp. basil, dried
- 2 tsp parsley, dried
- 3 cups vegetable stock
- 2 tbsp. tomato paste
- 1 tbsp. olive oil
- 1 medium onion, chopped
- Pepper
- Salt

Directions:

1. Add oil in instant pot and select sauté function.
2. Once oil is hot then add onion and sauté until soften.
3. Add tomato paste and stir for 2 minutes.
4. Now add all remaining ingredients except vinegar.
5. Seal pot with lid and cook on high for 10 minutes.
6. Release pressure using quick release method then open lid carefully.
7. Add balsamic vinegar and stir well.
8. Using blender puree the soup until creamy and smooth.
9. Serve hot and enjoy.

Nutritional Value (Amount per Serving):

- Calories 95
- Fat 4.1 g
- Carbohydrates 13.4 g
- Sugar 8.6 g
- Protein 3.1 g

Pumpkin Steel Cut Oatmeal

Serves: 4
Preparation Time: 15 minutes
Ingredients:

- 3/4 cup steel cut oats
- 1/2 tsp vanilla extract
- 1/2 tsp allspice
- 1 tsp ground cinnamon
- 3/4 cup pumpkin puree
- 2 1/4 cups water

Directions:

1. Add all ingredients into the instant pot and mix well.
2. Seal pot with lid and cook on high pressure for 3 minutes.
3. Allow to release pressure naturally then open lid.
4. Stir well and serve warm.

Nutritional Value (Amount per Serving):

- Calories 77
- Fat 1.2 g
- Carbohydrates 14.8 g
- Sugar 1.8 g
- Protein 2.6 g

Gluten Free Creamy Polenta

Serves: 3
Preparation Time: 30 minutes
Ingredients:

- 1/2 cup dry polenta, gluten free
- 1/2 tbsp. butter spread
- 1 cup almond milk
- 1 cup water
- 1/4 tsp salt

Directions:

1. Add almond milk, water and salt in instant pot and select sauté function.
2. Once liquid mixture is boil then add slowly polenta and stir well to combine.
3. Seal pot with lid and cook on manual high pressure for 5 minutes.
4. Allow to release pressure naturally then open lid.
5. Select sauté and cook until all liquid absorb.
6. Stir well and serve.

Nutritional Value (Amount per Serving):

- Calories 276
- Fat 19.3 g
- Carbohydrates 24.7 g
- Sugar 2.9 g
- Protein 3.8 g

Easy Black Bean Rice

Serves: 6
Preparation Time: 50 minutes
Ingredients:

- 2 cups rice
- 2 cups dried black beans
- 9 cups water
- 3 garlic cloves, minced
- 1 large onion, diced
- 1/2 tbsp. olive oil
- 1 tsp salt

Directions:

1. Add olive oil in instant pot and select sauté.
2. Once oil is hot then add onion and garlic and sauté until soften.
3. Add all remaining ingredients and mix well.
4. Seal pot with lid and select manual, press decrease arrows time to 27 minutes.
5. Allow to release pressure naturally then open lid.
6. Stir well and serve.

Nutritional Value (Amount per Serving):

- Calories 468
- Fat 2.5 g
- Carbohydrates 92.5 g
- Sugar 2.5 g
- Protein 18.8 g

Yummy Blueberry Oatmeal

Serves: 3
Preparation Time: 50 minutes
Ingredients:

- 1/2 cup blueberries
- 1 cup almond milk
- 1 cup quick oats
- 2 medium apples, peeled and diced
- 1 1/2 cups water
- 1/2 cups plain yogurt
- 2 tbsp. maple syrup
- 1/4 tsp ground nutmeg
- 1/4 tsp ground cinnamon
- 2 tbsp. vegan butter
- 1 tsp vanilla extract
- 1/4 tsp salt

Directions:

1. Grease bottom of instant pot container with butter.
2. Add blueberries, apples, water, yogurt, and oats, nutmeg and cinnamon in instant pot container. Mix well and soak overnight.
3. In the morning add salt and maple syrup and cook on porridge mode.
4. It takes about 20 minutes to get pressure and then 20 minutes to cook.
5. Release pressure using quick release method then open lid.
6. Add milk and vanilla.
7. Stir well and serve.

Nutritional Value (Amount per Serving):

- Calories 357
- Fat 12.2 g
- Carbohydrates 53.5 g
- Sugar 28.1 g
- Protein 9.3 g

Simple and Quick Risotto

Serves: 2
Preparation Time: 20 minutes
Ingredients:

- 1/2 cup Arborio rice
- 1 cup vegetable stock
- 1 tbsp. vegan butter, divided
- 2 tbsp. freshly chopped parsley
- 2 scallions, chopped
- 3 tsp white wine
- 1/4 tsp salt

Directions:

1. Melt half butter in instant pot using sauté function.
2. Add chopped parsley and scallions and sauté for 2 minutes.
3. Add rice and stir until rice edges begin to toast.
4. Add white wine, vegetable stock and salt stir well.
5. Seal pot with lid and cook on manual high pressure for 10 minutes.
6. Release pressure using quick release method then open lid carefully.
7. Add remaining butter stir until butter melted.
8. Serve hot and enjoy.

Nutritional Value (Amount per Serving):

- Calories 232
- Fat 6.3 g
- Carbohydrates 39.4 g
- Sugar 0 g
- Protein 3.7 g

Instant Spanish rice

Serves: 2
Preparation Time: 25 minutes
Ingredients:

- 1/2 cup rice
- 1/4 tsp pepper
- 1/4 tsp chili powder
- 1/2 bell pepper, chopped
- 1 tomato, chopped
- 3/4 cup vegetable stock
- 1 1/2 tbsp. tomato paste
- 1/2 onion, diced

Directions:

1. Add all ingredients into the instant pot.
2. Seal pot with lid and cook on high pressure for 8 minutes.
3. Allow to release pressure naturally then open lid.
4. Stir rice and serve.

Nutritional Value (Amount per Serving):

- Calories 206
- Fat 0.6 g
- Carbohydrates 45.6 g
- Sugar 5.0 g
- Protein 4.8 g

Slow Cook Plain Brown Rice

Serves: 6
Preparation Time: 25 minutes
Ingredients:

- 2 cups brown rice
- 2 1/2 cups water

Directions:

1. Add water and rice in instant pot.
2. Seal pot with lid and cook on high for 22 minutes.
3. Release pressure using quick release method then open lid carefully.
4. Serve warm and enjoy.

Nutritional Value (Amount per Serving):

- Calories 229
- Fat 1.7 g
- Carbohydrates 48.2 g
- Sugar 0 g
- Protein 4.8 g

Delicious Instant Pot Quinoa

Serves: 4
Preparation Time: 15 minutes
Ingredients:

- 2 cups quinoa, rinse
- 2 tbsp. fresh parsley, chopped
- 1 fresh lemon juice
- 3 cups water
- 1/4 tsp salt

Directions:

1. Add all ingredients into the instant pot.
2. Seal pot with lid and cook on high pressure for 1 minute.
3. Allow to release pressure naturally then open lid.

4. Serve warm and enjoy.

Nutritional Value (Amount per Serving):

- Calories 314
- Fat 5.2 g
- Carbohydrates 54.7 g
- Sugar 0 g
- Protein 12.1 g

Gluten Free Coconut Oatmeal

Serves: 6

Preparation Time: 15 minutes

Ingredients:

- 2 cups oats
- 2 tbsp. coconut sugar
- 1/2 tsp ground cinnamon
- 1/4 tsp vanilla extract
- 4 cups coconut milk, unsweetened
- 1/4 salt

Directions:

1. Add all ingredients into the instant pot and mix well.
2. Seal pot with lid and cook on high pressure for 4 minutes.
3. Allow to release pressure naturally then open lid.
4. Stir well and serve.

Nutritional Value (Amount per Serving):

- Calories 472
- Fat 39.9 g
- Carbohydrates 27.5 g
- Sugar 5.6 g
- Protein 7.3 g

Delicious Vegetable Pasta

Serves: 4

Preparation Time: 20 minutes

Ingredients:

- 16 oz. pasta
- 10 oz. organic broccoli
- 25 oz. tomato puree
- 4 cups water

Directions:

1. Add all ingredients into the instant pot and mix well to combine.
2. Seal pot with lid and cook on manual high pressure for 6 minutes.
3. Release pressure using quick release method then open lid carefully.
4. Stir well and serve.

Nutritional Value (Amount per Serving):

- Calories 418
- Fat 3.2 g
- Carbohydrates 82.7 g
- Sugar 9.8 g
- Protein 17.7 g

Fast Vegetable Gumbo

Serves: 4
Preparation Time: 20 minutes
Ingredients:

- 2 cups vegetable stock
- 2 tbsp. tamari sauce
- 2 medium zucchini, sliced
- 3 garlic cloves, chopped
- 1 cup mushrooms, sliced
- 1 cup kidney beans, soaked overnight
- 1 bell pepper, chopped
- 2 tbsp. extra virgin olive oil

Directions:

1. Add all ingredients into the instant pot and mix well.
2. Seal pot with lid and cook on high pressure for 8 minutes,
3. Allow to release pressure naturally then open lid.
4. Stir well and serve.

Nutritional Value (Amount per Serving):

- Calories 254
- Fat 7.9 g
- Carbohydrates 36.1 g
- Sugar 5.3 g
- Protein 13.0 g

Delicious Garlic Potato Mash

Serves: 4
Preparation Time: 20 minutes
Ingredients:

- 4 russet potatoes, peeled and diced
- 4 tbsp. parsley, chopped
- 1/2 cup soy milk
- 5 garlic cloves, chopped
- 1 cup vegetable broth
- Salt

Directions:

1. Add garlic, potatoes and vegetable broth in instant pot.
2. Seal pot with lid and cook on high pressure for 4 minutes.
3. Release pressure using quick release method then open lid carefully.
4. Transfer potatoes in bowl and add soy milk.
5. Using masher mash the potatoes.
6. Add parsley and salt. Mix well.
7. Serve warm and enjoy.

Nutritional Value (Amount per Serving):

- Calories 179
- Fat 1.1 g
- Carbohydrates 36.9 g
- Sugar 3.9 g
- Protein 6.0 g

Instant Breakfast Quinoa

Serves: 6
Preparation Time: 15 minutes
Ingredients:

- 1 1/2 cups quinoa, uncooked and rinsed
- 2 tbsp. maple syrup
- 2 1/4 cups water
- 1/2 tsp vanilla
- 1/4 tsp ground cinnamon
- Sliced almonds

Directions:

1. Add water, quinoa, vanilla, maple syrup, cinnamon and salt in instant pot.
2. Seal pot with lid and cook on high pressure for 1 minute.
3. Release pressure using quick release method then open lid carefully.
4. Stir and serve with sliced almonds.

Nutritional Value (Amount per Serving):

- Calories 176
- Fat 2.2 g
- Carbohydrates 32.0 g
- Sugar 4.2 g
- Protein 6.1 g

Slow Cook Maple Glazed Carrot

Serves: 4

Preparation Time: 15 minutes

Ingredients:

- 1 lbs. carrots, peeled and sliced
- 1 tbsp. vegan butter
- 1 cup water
- 3 tbsp. raisins
- 1 tbsp. maple syrup
- 1/2 tsp pepper

Directions:

1. Add water, carrots and raisins in instant pot.
2. Seal pot with lid and cook on high for 3 minutes.
3. Release pressure using quick release method then open lid carefully.
4. Drained carrot and transfer in bowl.
5. Add butter and maple syrup in bowl and toss well until butter is melted.
6. Season with black pepper.
7. Serve and enjoy.

Nutritional Value (Amount per Serving):

- Calories 105
- Fat 2.9 g
- Carbohydrates 19.9 g
- Sugar 12.6 g
- Protein 1.2 g

Instant Homemade Salsa

Serves: 6
Preparation Time: 40 minutes
Ingredients:

- 12 cups fresh tomatoes, peeled, seeded and diced
- 6 oz. tomato paste
- 1/2 cup jalapeno peppers, seeded and chopped
- 3 medium onion, chopped
- 2 large green peppers, chopped
- 4 tbsp. cilantro
- 2 tbsp. cayenne pepper
- 1 1/2 tbsp. garlic powder
- 2 tbsp. raw cane sugar
- 1/2 cup vinegar
- 1 tbsp. salt

Directions:

1. Add all ingredients into the instant pot and mix well to combine.
2. Seal pot with lid and cook on high for 30 minutes.
3. Allow to release pressure naturally then open lid.
4. Allow to cool completely then serve.

Nutritional Value (Amount per Serving):

- Calories 140
- Fat 1.4 g
- Carbohydrates 30.2 g
- Sugar 17.5 g
- Protein 6.1 g

Instant Spinach Artichoke Dip

Serves: 8
Preparation Time: 15 minutes
Ingredients:

- 10 oz. spinach, frozen
- 15 oz. artichoke hearts
- 1 tsp onion powder
- 2 garlic cloves
- 1/2 cup mayonnaise
- 1/2 cup vegan sour cream
- 1/2 cup vegetable broth
- 8 oz. vegan mozzarella cheese, shredded
- 14 oz. vegan parmesan cheese, shredded
- 8 oz. vegan cream cheese

Directions:

1. Add all ingredients except cheese into the instant pot and mix well to combine.
2. Seal pot with lid and cook on high for 5 minutes.
3. Release pressure using quick release method then open lid carefully.
4. Add cheese and stir well until cheese melted.
5. Serve and enjoy.

Nutritional Value (Amount per Serving):

- Calories 455
- Fat 33.7 g
- Carbohydrates 12.2 g
- Sugar 1.8 g
- Protein 28.9 g

Healthy Vegetable Stew

Serves: 4
Preparation Time: 30 minutes
Ingredients:

- 1 1/2 lbs. potatoes, peeled and cut into 1 inch pieces
- 2 large carrots, peeled and sliced
- 1 celery rib, sliced
- 1 leek, sliced
- 1 tsp olive oil
- 1 tbsp. flour, dissolve in 1 tbsp. water
- 1/2 tsp Worcestershire sauce
- 1 portabella mushroom, diced
- 1/2 tsp herb de Provence
- 2 cups vegetable stock
- 1/2 cup frozen peas
- 1/4 tsp pepper
- 1/4 tsp salt

Directions:

1. Add olive oil and mushroom in instant pot and select sauté for 2 minutes.
2. Add celery, potatoes, carrots, Worcestershire sauce, herbs, vegetable stock, pepper and salt. Stir well.
3. Seal pot with lid and select stew mode and set timer for 10 minutes.
4. Allow to release pressure naturally then open lid carefully.
5. Add flour slurry and frozen peas. Stir well and set sauté function for 1 minute.
6. Serve warm and enjoy.

Nutritional Value (Amount per Serving):

- Calories 120
- Fat 1.4 g
- Carbohydrates 24.9 g
- Sugar 5.3 g
- Protein 3.5 g

Slow Cook Spinach Lentil Curry

Serves: 6
Preparation Time: 30 minutes
Ingredients:

- 1 1/2 cups red lentils, dried
- 4 cups baby spinach, chopped
- 1 medium onion, chopped
- 2 tbsp. olive oil
- 1/4 tsp cayenne pepper
- 1 tsp ground turmeric
- 1 tsp ground coriander
- 1 tsp ground cumin
- 1/4 cup cilantro, chopped
- 1 medium potato, diced
- 3 cups vegetable stock
- 3 garlic cloves, minced
- 1/2 tsp salt

Directions:

1. Add olive oil and onion in instant pot and select sauté for 5 minutes.
2. Add garlic stir well and sauté for 30 seconds.
3. Add cayenne pepper, turmeric, coriander and cumin. Mix well to combine.
4. Add potato, vegetable stock, lentils and salt. Stir well.
5. Seal pot with lid and cook on high for 10 minutes.
6. Release pressure using quick release method then open lid.
7. Add cilantro and spinach. Stir well.
8. Serve hot with rice.

Nutritional Value (Amount per Serving):

- Calories 275
- Fat 5.2 g
- Carbohydrates 43.0 g
- Sugar 2.1 g
- Protein 14.9 g

Delicious Almond Coconut Risotto

Serves: 4
Preparation Time: 25 minutes
Ingredients:

- 1 cup Arborio rice
- 2 tbsp. almonds, sliced and toasted
- 2 tbsp. coconut flakes, sliced and toasted
- 1 tsp vanilla extract
- 1/3 cup coconut sugar
- 1 cup coconut milk
- 2 cups almond milk

Directions:

1. Add coconut milk and almond milk in instant pot and select sauté function.
2. Once milk is boil then add rice and stir well.
3. Seal pot with lid and cook on high for 5 minutes.
4. Allow to release pressure naturally then open lid.
5. Now add all remaining ingredients and stir well to combine.
6. Serve warm and enjoy.

Nutritional Value (Amount per Serving):

- Calories 614
- Fat 45.5 g
- Carbohydrates 48.9 g
- Sugar 6.4 g
- Protein 8.0 g

Instant Mixed Vegetable Curry

Serves: 6

Preparation Time: 6 hours 10 minutes

Ingredients:

- 1 cup chickpeas, soaked overnight
- 2 cups butternut squash, cubed
- 1 tbsp. garlic powder
- 1 tsp chili powder
- 1 tbsp. cumin powder
- 2 cups vegetable broth
- 1 cup kale, chopped
- 2 cups coconut milk
- 3 garlic cloves, chopped
- 1 medium onion, chopped
- 3 tbsp. olive oil
- 1 tsp pepper

Directions:

1. Add all ingredients into the instant pot and mix well.
2. Seal pot with lid and select slow cooker function for 6 hours.
3. Serve warm with rice.

Nutritional Value (Amount per Serving):

- Calories 425
- Fat 28.9 g
- Carbohydrates 35.7 g
- Sugar 8.7 g
- Protein 11.5 g

Delicious Potato Risotto

Serves: 4
Preparation Time: 25 minutes
Ingredients:

- 2 cups rice
- 1 tbsp. tomato paste
- 4 cups vegetable stock
- 1 medium potato, cubed
- 4 tbsp. white wine
- 1 medium onion, chopped
- 1 tbsp. olive oil
- 1 tsp salt

Directions:

1. Add olive oil and onion in instant pot and select sauté for 4 minutes.
2. Add rice and stir for 2 minutes.
3. Add white wine and stir until rice absorbs wine.
4. Add vegetable stock, potatoes, tomato paste and salt. Stir.
5. Seal pot with lid and cook on high for 5 minutes.
6. Allow to release pressure naturally then open lid.
7. Serve warm and enjoy.

Nutritional Value (Amount per Serving):

- Calories 442
- Fat 4.5 g
- Carbohydrates 88.4 g
- Sugar 2.3 g
- Protein 8.0 g

Instant Slow Cook Carrot Soup

Serves: 5

Preparation Time: 20 minutes

Ingredients:

- 1lb carrot, peeled and chopped
- 4 cups vegetable stock
- 1/2 cup coconut milk
- 1/4 tsp ground turmeric
- 1 tsp curry powder
- 1 tsp garlic powder
- 1 tsp fresh ginger, grated
- 1 onion, chopped
- 1 tbsp. olive oil
- 1/4 tsp cayenne pepper
- 1/2 tsp salt

Directions:

1. Add olive oil and onion in instant pot and sauté for 5 minutes.
2. Add carrots and sauté for 3 minutes.
3. Add vegetable stock, turmeric, curry powder, garlic powder, salt, ginger and cayenne pepper. Stir well.
4. Seal pot with lid and cook on high for 10 minutes.
5. Release pressure using quick release method then open lid carefully.
6. Using blender puree the soup.
7. Add coconut milk stir well and serve.

Nutritional Value (Amount per Serving):

- Calories 130
- Fat 8.6 g
- Carbohydrates 13.4 g
- Sugar 6.4 g
- Protein 1.7 g

Conclusion

Thank you again for reading this book!

As you can see, the benefits of incorporating a healthy diet and the instant pot cooker helps to create simple, delicious meals that pack a nutrient punch.

The most important thing about approaching a healthy lifestyle is ensuring that you're eating enough and you are eating the right things. The right things include foods that are going to optimize your body for top performance so you can consume and move throughout your day with ease.

As with any change in lifestyle comes the challenge to stick with your decision to try something new. The next step is to make some more of these recipes if you've only made a few of them. You just might find a new favorite!

To your health!

Anthony Marshall

Made in the USA
Middletown, DE
23 August 2017